The HEIRS™ Guide to
Generational Wealth

THE HEIRS™ GUIDE TO GENERATIONAL WEALTH

Faith-Driven Strategies to Build Wealth,

Claim Your Promise, and Create a Legacy

KITO J. JOHNSON

Published by Melchizedek Global Publishing

Printed in the United States of America.

Some names and identifying details have been changed to protect the privacy of individuals. Certain stories and examples are composites or have been adapted for illustrative purposes.

ISBN: 978-0-9989502-5-9

First Edition

DEDICATION

To every person who has ever dared to believe that God has more in store for them and their family.

This book is for the builders, the dreamers, and the faithful who refuse to settle.

Your legacy starts now.

C O N T E N T S

INTRODUCTION

Welcome to The HEIRS™ Guide to Generational Wealth. If you're reading these words, something inside you is stirring. Maybe it's a desire for financial freedom. Maybe it's a vision for your family's future. Maybe it's a quiet knowing that God has called you to build something that lasts far beyond your own lifetime.

Whatever brought you here, I believe it's not a coincidence. I believe God has placed this book in your hands for a reason.

Before we go any further, I want you to understand the spiritual foundation this entire book is built on. The HEIRS™ framework is not something I invented out of thin air. It's rooted in two foundational scriptures that anchor everything you're about to read.

The first is Genesis 13:14–15: "Lift up your eyes... for all the land which you see, to you will I give it, and to your seed forever." This is the original promise God made to Abraham. It establishes land ownership as part of a divine inheritance—not just a financial opportunity, but a God-given assignment. Ownership begins with vision and a promise.

The second is Galatians 3:29: "And if ye be Christ's, then are ye Abraham's seed, and heirs according to the promise." This connects every believer today directly back to Abraham. It confirms that the promise of inheritance—including land—extends beyond the Old Testament and applies right now, to you.

Genesis establishes the promise. Galatians confirms who inherits it. Together, they form the spiritual foundation of The HEIRS™, positioning real estate ownership as part of a larger assignment tied to inheritance and legacy. That's not just a financial strategy—that's a calling.

This is not your average personal finance book. You won't find generic advice about cutting lattes and saving pennies. What you will find is a comprehensive, faith-driven roadmap for building real, lasting, generational wealth—the kind of wealth that changes your family tree forever.

This book is organized into three parts. Part One focuses on mindset—because before you can build wealth externally, you have to build it internally. You'll learn how to think like an heir, act in faith, break generational cycles, and master the fundamentals of financial literacy.

Part Two is all about strategy. This is where we get into the nuts and bolts of wealth-building—real estate investing, multiple income streams, creative financing, and asset protection. These are the practical tools you'll use to build your financial empire.

Part Three is about legacy. Building wealth is only half the equation. Transferring it to the next generation—with the wisdom and values to sustain it—is the other half. You'll learn how to teach your children, build as a family, leverage community, give generously, and create a plan that extends one hundred years into the future.

Throughout every chapter, I'll share personal stories, practical strategies, and biblical principles that have guided my own journey from broke and uncertain to financially free and purpose-driven.

I want to be clear about one thing: I'm not writing to you from a place of perfection. I'm writing from a place of experience. I've made mistakes. I've lost money. I've made decisions I wish I could take back. But through it all, God has been faithful. He's taught me through every failure and blessed me through every step of obedience. And I believe He'll do the same for you.

So here's what I need from you: commitment. Commit to reading this book from cover to cover. Commit to doing the exercises. Commit to taking action—even when it's uncomfortable. Because the distance between where you are and where God wants to take you is bridged by action.

You are an heir to the promises of God. It's time to claim your inheritance.

Let's go.

PART ONE: MINDSET — BECOMING AN HEIR

CHAPTER 1

You Were Born to Build

"For I know the plans I have for you," declares the Lord, "plans to prosper you and not to harm you, plans to give you hope and a future." — Jeremiah 29:11

I remember sitting in my grandmother's kitchen as a kid, watching her count out dollars from an envelope she kept tucked behind the sugar jar. She wasn't rich by the world's standards. She didn't drive a fancy car or live in a gated community. But she owned her home. She had food on the table every single night. And every Sunday, she put something in the offering plate at church without a second thought.

What my grandmother understood—even if she never used the word—was stewardship. She knew that everything she had was a gift from God, and she treated it that way. She didn't waste. She didn't complain about what she didn't have. She managed what was in her hands with wisdom and faithfulness.

That image has stayed with me my entire life. And it's the reason I wrote this book.

If you're holding this book right now, it's not by accident. I believe God placed it in your hands because you're ready. You're ready to stop surviving and start building. You're ready to stop hoping things get better and start making them better. You're ready to become the heir God has already declared you to be.

Here's what you need to know right from the start: wealth is not just about money. It never has been. Wealth is about freedom. It's about options. It's about being able to say yes to the things that matter and no to the things that don't. Wealth is about creating a life where your children and your children's children don't have to start from scratch. That's what generational wealth really means.

And the truth is, God wants this for you. The Bible is full of promises about abundance, provision, and blessing. From Abraham to Solomon to the parable of the talents, Scripture makes it clear: God is not opposed to wealth. He's opposed to the love of money. He's opposed to greed. But He is absolutely in favor of His people being blessed, being prosperous, and using their resources to advance His kingdom.

So if you've ever felt guilty about wanting more—more income, more security, more opportunity—let me free you from that right now. Wanting more is not selfish. Wanting more so you can do more, give more, and bless more is exactly what God designed you for.

Redefining Wealth Through a Faith Lens

The world has a very specific definition of wealth. It usually involves a number—a net worth figure, a bank account balance, or the size of a stock portfolio. And while those things matter, they're only part of the picture.

When I talk about wealth in this book, I'm talking about something bigger. I'm talking about wholeness. I'm talking about a life that's rich in purpose, rich in relationships, rich in health, and yes—rich in finances. Because here's the bottom line: if you have a million dollars in the bank but your family is falling apart, you're not wealthy. If you own ten properties but you're spiritually bankrupt, you're not wealthy. True wealth is holistic.

That's why faith has to be at the center of everything we do. When you build wealth with God as your foundation, it doesn't just change your bank account—it changes your life. It changes the way you think about money, the way you treat people, and the way you make decisions. It keeps you grounded when the numbers go up and it keeps you hopeful when the numbers go down.

Proverbs 10:22 says, "The blessing of the Lord brings wealth, without painful toil for it." Now, that doesn't mean you don't have to work hard. It means that when God is in it, the work produces fruit. It means your labor is not in vain. It means the hustle has purpose and the grind has direction.

I've seen this in my own life. When I first got into real estate, I was hustling like crazy—but I was doing it my way. I was cutting corners, chasing deals without praying about them, and making decisions based on fear instead of faith. And you know what happened? I burned out. I made bad deals. I lost money.

But when I surrendered my business to God—when I started praying before every deal, tithing off my profits, and seeking wisdom from mentors who walked with the Lord—everything shifted. Not overnight. Not without challenges. But the trajectory changed. The fruit started showing up. And it's been growing ever since.

That's the kind of wealth I want for you. Not just financial prosperity, but a blessed life that reflects the goodness of God in every area.

The HEIRS™ Framework

Before we go any further, let me break down the framework that this entire book is built on. I call it The HEIRS™ framework. It's rooted in two scriptures: Genesis 13:14–15, where God told Abraham, "Lift up your eyes... for all the land which you see, to you will I give it, and to your seed forever," and Galatians 3:29, which confirms, "If ye be Christ's, then are ye Abraham's seed, and heirs according to the promise." Genesis establishes the promise. Galatians confirms who inherits it. And The HEIRS™ framework is how you walk it out. It stands for five principles that will guide you from where you are to where God is calling you to be.

H — Honor God First. Everything starts with putting God at the center of your financial life. That means tithing, praying over your finances, and making decisions that align with His Word. When you honor God with your first fruits, He opens doors you didn't even know existed.

E — Educate Yourself Relentlessly. Financial literacy is not optional—it's essential. You can't build what you don't understand. This book will give you a strong foundation, but your education should never stop. Read books. Take courses. Find mentors. The more you know, the more you grow.

I — Invest with Intention. Don't just save money—put it to work. Whether it's real estate, stocks, a business, or all three, your money should be producing more money. Investing is how you go from working for a living to having your money work for you.

R — Repeat and Scale. Once you find a strategy that works, do it again. And again. And again. Wealth is not built on one lucky break—it's built on consistent, repeated action. Scale what works. Drop what doesn't. Keep moving forward.

S — Steward the Legacy. This is the part most people forget. Building wealth is only half the battle. The other half is making sure it lasts beyond your lifetime. That means teaching your children, setting up trusts, creating systems, and living in a way that inspires the next generation to keep building.

If you take nothing else away from this book, take this: you are an heir. Not just spiritually, but practically. God has given you the ability, the creativity, and the opportunity to build something that lasts. The question is—will you step into it?

This is your moment. Don't let it pass you by.

Why I Wrote This Book

Let me be real with you for a second. I didn't write this book because I have it all figured out. I wrote it because I've been exactly where you are. I've been broke. I've been in debt. I've been the person lying awake at night wondering how I was going to make it.

I stumbled into my first real estate deal at just twenty years old. I didn't come from money. I didn't have a trust fund or a rich uncle. What I had was a willingness to learn, a refusal to stay stuck, and a God who kept opening doors when I had no business walking through them.

Over the years, I've built a real estate portfolio, mentored hundreds of people, and watched God do things in my finances that I never could have imagined. But I've also made mistakes—big ones. I've lost deals. I've trusted the wrong people. I've let fear hold me back when I should have moved forward.

Every lesson in this book comes from real life. My life. The lives of people I've coached. The principles I've learned from Scripture and from the trenches of building wealth in the real world.

I wrote this book for the single mom who's working two jobs and wondering if there's a better way. I wrote it for the young professional who's making decent money but has no idea how to make it grow. I wrote it for the couple who loves the Lord but feels stuck financially. I wrote it for anyone who's ever looked at their bank account and thought, "There has to be more than this."

There is. And you're about to discover it.

So here's my challenge to you before you turn another page: commit. Commit to reading this book all the way through. Commit to doing the exercises at the end of each chapter. Commit to taking action, even when it's uncomfortable. Because knowledge without action is just information. But knowledge plus action? That's transformation.

Let's build something together. Let's build something that lasts. Let's build a legacy.

Trust the process. God's got you.

The Cost of Doing Nothing

Let me paint a picture for you. Imagine two people. Both are thirty years old. Both earn the same salary. Both come from similar backgrounds. The only difference is that one of them starts investing five hundred dollars a month today, and the other one waits ten years to start.

By the time they both turn sixty, the person who started at thirty has over a million dollars. The person who waited until forty? They have less than half of that. Same income. Same amount invested per month. The only difference is time.

That's the cost of doing nothing. Every year you wait, you're not just losing time—you're losing the compounding effect of that time. Albert Einstein reportedly called compound interest the eighth wonder of the world. And he wasn't exaggerating.

But here's the thing—this principle doesn't just apply to money. It applies to knowledge, relationships, and habits. Every day you wait to learn about investing is a day of knowledge you'll never get back. Every month you delay building your network is a month of missed connections and opportunities. Every year you put off teaching your children about money is a year of financial habits they're forming without your guidance.

The enemy of generational wealth is not failure. It's inaction. It's the belief that there's always tomorrow. But tomorrow isn't promised—and even if it were, tomorrow's dollar is worth less than today's.

So I'll ask you again: are you ready? Because the clock is ticking, the opportunity is here, and God is waiting for you to step into what He's prepared. Don't let another day pass without taking action. Your children's children are depending on what you do right now.

Reflection and Action Steps

Before you move on to the next chapter, I want you to pause and do something. Get a notebook—a physical notebook, not your phone—and write down your answers to these questions.

First, what does wealth mean to you? Not the dictionary definition—your personal definition. What would your life look like if you were truly wealthy? Think about your family, your time, your giving, your purpose. Write it all down.

Second, what beliefs about money did you grow up with? Were they empowering or limiting? Write down at least three messages you received about money as a child—from your parents, your community, your church. Then next to each one, write down what you now believe to be true based on God's Word.

Third, write down one specific financial goal you want to accomplish in the next ninety days. Make it measurable. Make it realistic. And make it meaningful. Maybe it's saving your first one thousand dollars. Maybe it's pulling your credit report. Maybe it's reading two more books on investing. Whatever it is, write it down, put a date on it, and commit to it.

This exercise might seem simple, but don't skip it. The act of writing crystallizes your thinking, solidifies your commitment, and creates a record you can look back on. Some of the most successful people I've mentored point back to a single moment when they wrote down their goals as the turning point in their journey.

Your turning point is right now. Pick up that pen.

A New Definition of Success

The world measures success by what you accumulate. God measures success by what you steward. And that distinction will change everything about the way you approach wealth.

I used to chase numbers. I thought if I could just hit a certain net worth or close a certain number of deals, I'd feel successful. But every time I hit a milestone, the goalpost moved. The number was never enough. The achievement was never satisfying. And I realized I was chasing the wrong thing.

True success isn't about accumulation—it's about impact. It's about the lives you change, the people you mentor, the community you strengthen, and the legacy you leave. When you redefine success through a kingdom lens, you stop comparing yourself to others and start measuring yourself against your own purpose.

Ask yourself: am I using what God has given me to make a difference? Am I growing, learning, and getting better every day? Am I positioning my family for generational blessing? If the answer is yes, then you're succeeding—regardless of what your bank account says today.

Wealth is a tool. Success is a life well-lived. And when you get that distinction clear in your mind, you'll find a peace and a motivation that numbers alone can never provide.

The Three Pillars of Generational Wealth

Before we dive into the strategies and tactics in the rest of this book, I want to establish three pillars that every wealth-building plan must rest on. Without these pillars, even the best strategy will crumble.

The first pillar is spiritual alignment. Your wealth-building journey must be surrendered to God. That doesn't mean you passively wait for Him to drop money into your lap. It means you invite Him into your planning, your decision-making, and your execution. You pray before you buy. You seek His wisdom before you invest. You tithe before you spend. When God is your partner, you have access to supernatural wisdom, divine connections, and opportunities that defy human logic.

The second pillar is financial intelligence. Knowledge is the bridge between desire and results. You can want wealth all day long, but without understanding how money works—how it's earned, grown, protected, and transferred—desire alone won't get you there. Every chapter in this book is designed to raise your financial intelligence. But don't stop here. Read other books. Take courses. Attend seminars. Make financial education a lifelong habit.

The third pillar is consistent execution. Ideas without action are just fantasies. Plans without follow-through are just paperwork. The people who build lasting wealth are not necessarily the smartest or the most talented. They're the most consistent. They show up every day. They do the boring, unglamorous work. They keep going when it's hard, when it's slow, and when nobody's watching.

Spiritual alignment, financial intelligence, and consistent execution. When these three pillars are in place, your wealth-building house is built to last. And no storm—financial or otherwise—can take it down.

CHAPTER 2

The HEIRS' Mindset

"As a man thinks in his heart, so is he." — Proverbs 23:7

Have you ever noticed that the people who build wealth tend to think differently than the people who don't? It's not that they're smarter. It's not that they work harder. And it's definitely not that they're luckier. The difference is in their mindset.

I used to think that getting rich was about finding the right opportunity at the right time. I thought if I could just land the perfect deal or meet the right person, everything would fall into place. But the more I grew in my faith and in my financial education, the more I realized something: the opportunity was never the problem. My thinking was the problem.

You see, most of us were raised with a scarcity mindset. We grew up hearing things like, "Money doesn't grow on trees." "We can't afford that." "Rich people are greedy." And while those statements might have been well-intentioned, they planted seeds of limitation in our minds. Seeds that grew into beliefs. Beliefs that became barriers.

If you believe money is hard to come by, you'll always struggle to make it. If you believe rich people are bad, you'll subconsciously sabotage your own success. If you believe you can't afford things, you'll never look for ways to make them affordable. Your mindset creates your reality.

That's why the first step to building generational wealth isn't opening a brokerage account or buying a house. The first step is changing the way you think.

Breaking Poverty Thinking

Poverty thinking is sneaky. It doesn't always look like what you'd expect. You can have a six-figure salary and still have a poverty mindset. You can drive a nice car and still think like someone who's broke. Poverty thinking isn't about how much money you have—it's about how you relate to money.

Here are some signs of a poverty mindset. See if any of these sound familiar. You spend money the moment you get it because you're afraid it won't last. You feel guilty about wanting nice things. You avoid looking at your bank account because it stresses you out. You believe that wealthy people must have done something shady to get there. You think investing is "too risky" or "not for people like me."

If any of that resonated, don't feel bad. I've been there. Most of us have. The important thing is that you recognize it so you can start to change it.

The Bible tells us in Romans 12:2 to "be transformed by the renewing of your mind." That's not just a spiritual principle—it's a financial one. If you want to transform your finances, you have to transform your thinking first.

So how do you do that? It starts with awareness. Pay attention to the thoughts you have about money. When you see something you want, what's your first thought? When someone talks about investing, what's your internal reaction? When you think about the future, do you feel hope or dread?

Once you become aware of your thought patterns, you can start to replace the lies with truth. Instead of "I can't afford that," try asking, "How can I afford that?" Instead of "Investing is too risky," try saying, "I'm going to learn how to invest wisely." Instead of "Wealth isn't for people like me," declare, "God has called me to be a good steward of abundance."

This isn't just positive thinking—it's biblical thinking. You're aligning your mind with what God has already said about you.

Claiming God's Promises Over Your Finances

One of the most powerful things you can do for your financial life is to get into the Word of God and find out what He says about provision, blessing, and abundance. Because when you know what God has promised, you can stand on those promises even when your circumstances don't match up yet.

Let me give you a few to get started. Philippians 4:19 says, "And my God will meet all your needs according to the riches of his glory in Christ Jesus." Deuteronomy 8:18 says, "Remember the Lord your God, for it is he who gives you the ability to produce wealth." Malachi 3:10 says, "Bring the whole tithe into the storehouse, that there may be food in my house. Test me in this, and see if I will not throw open the floodgates of heaven and pour out so much blessing that there will not be room enough to store it."

These aren't just nice verses to put on a coffee mug. These are promises from the Creator of the universe. And if God said it, He means it. But here's the thing—promises require participation. God's provision is available, but you have to position yourself to receive it.

That means you can't just pray for wealth and then sit on the couch. You have to pray and then move. You have to believe and then act. You have to trust God and then do the work.

I've seen this play out so many times in my own journey. There were deals that made no sense on paper, but I felt God leading me into them. There were moments when I had to write a check that terrified me, but I knew God was saying, "Trust me." And every single time I obeyed, He showed up.

Now, I'm not telling you to be reckless. I'm telling you to be faithful. There's a difference. Recklessness ignores wisdom. Faith operates in partnership with wisdom. When you seek God first, He gives you the discernment to know what to do and the courage to do it.

So start claiming those promises. Write them down. Speak them over your finances. Pray them over your family. Because when your mind is renewed by the Word of God, your actions change. And when your actions change, your results change. And when your results change, your legacy changes.

Identity: You Are an Heir

Here's something that changed everything for me: understanding my identity in Christ. Galatians 3:29 says, "If you belong to Christ, then you are Abraham's seed, and heirs according to the promise."

Do you understand what that means? You are an heir. Not because of what you've done, but because of whose you are. The same God who blessed Abraham with wealth beyond measure, the same God who made Joseph the second most powerful man in Egypt, the same God who gave Solomon wisdom and riches—that God is your Father. And you are His heir.

When you truly grasp this, it changes how you carry yourself. It changes what you tolerate. It changes what you expect. An heir doesn't beg for scraps—an heir walks in the fullness of what's been prepared for them. An heir doesn't settle for less—an heir takes possession of the promise.

Now, I'm not talking about some name-it-and-claim-it theology where you just declare a Bentley into your driveway. I'm talking about a deep, rooted understanding that God has equipped you to build, to create, and to leave a legacy. That understanding doesn't make you entitled—it makes you responsible. Because with great blessing comes great stewardship.

So here's my challenge to you: start seeing yourself the way God sees you. Not as someone who's barely getting by, but as someone who's been called to thrive. Not as someone who's disqualified because of past mistakes, but as someone who's been redeemed and repositioned for purpose. Not as someone who's hoping for a break, but as someone who's building a legacy.

You are an heir. Now it's time to start living like one.

Don't miss this. Your identity drives your decisions. Your decisions shape your actions. Your actions determine your outcomes. And your outcomes define your legacy. It all starts with knowing who you are.

This is your moment. Step into it.

Rewiring Your Financial Identity

Changing your mindset isn't a one-time event—it's a daily discipline. Just like you have to exercise your body consistently to stay in shape, you have to exercise your mind consistently to stay in a wealth-building posture.

Here are some practices that have helped me and the people I mentor rewire their financial identity. First, start your day with declarations. Before your feet hit the floor, speak God's promises over your life. Declare that you are blessed. Declare that you are a good steward. Declare that God is opening doors for you. This isn't wishful thinking—it's warfare. You're combating years of negative programming with the truth of God's Word.

Second, audit your inputs. What are you listening to? What are you watching? Who are you spending time with? If your daily inputs are filled with negativity, scarcity thinking, and people who complain about money, your mindset will reflect that. But if you fill your mind with financial education, success stories, and the Word of God, your thinking will begin to shift.

Third, celebrate small wins. Most people only celebrate the big milestones—the first property, the six-figure income, the paid-off mortgage. But the journey to those milestones is paved with hundreds of small wins that deserve recognition. Did you save an extra hundred dollars this month? Celebrate it. Did you resist an impulse purchase? Celebrate it. Did you read a chapter of a finance book? Celebrate it. Small wins build confidence, and confidence fuels bigger action.

Fourth, surround yourself with abundance thinkers. I can't stress this enough. You become the average of the five people you spend the most time with. If those five people are broke, frustrated, and making excuses, you'll adopt those patterns. But if those five people are investing, growing, and trusting God with bold moves, you'll rise to that level.

Your mindset is not fixed. It's flexible. And with intentional effort, you can transform the way you think about money, wealth, and your God-given potential. It starts today. It starts with you choosing, every single day, to think like the heir God says you are.

Reflection and Action Steps

Here's your assignment for this chapter. Take out your notebook and answer these questions honestly.

First, write down three limiting beliefs you have about money. Be honest—nobody is going to see this but you. Then next to each belief, write a truth from Scripture that contradicts it. For example, if your limiting belief is "I'll never be wealthy," write Deuteronomy 8:18 next to it: "God gives me the ability to produce wealth."

Second, identify one person in your life who has the kind of financial mindset you want to develop. Reach out to them this week. Ask them to coffee. Ask them about their journey. Ask them what shifted in their thinking. You'd be surprised how willing successful people are to share their stories when you approach them with genuine curiosity and humility.

Third, for the next thirty days, start each morning by reading one financial Scripture and making one positive declaration about your finances. It takes less than two minutes, but the cumulative effect is powerful.

Your mindset is the soil in which everything else grows. Tend to it with care, feed it with truth, and protect it from weeds. Because when the soil is right, the harvest is inevitable.

The Thermostat Principle

Here's a concept that blew my mind when I first heard it: most people have a financial thermostat. Just like the thermostat in your house is set to a certain temperature, your subconscious mind is set to a certain financial level. And no matter what happens externally, you'll always gravitate back to that setting.

This is why lottery winners often go broke within a few years. Their external circumstances changed dramatically, but their internal thermostat didn't. They were still programmed for the same financial level they'd always known. So they spent, gave, and wasted until they were right back where they started.

It's also why some people can lose everything and build it back. Their thermostat is set high. They've internalized the identity of a wealth-builder, so even when circumstances knock them down, they get back up and rebuild.

So the question is: what is your financial thermostat set to? And how do you raise it?

You raise it through education—the more you learn about wealth, the more normal it becomes in your mind. You raise it through exposure—spending time with people who operate at higher financial levels expands your sense of what's possible. You raise it through experience—every deal you close, every investment you make, and every financial win you achieve raises your internal setting. And you raise it through faith—declaring God's promises over your life and believing that He has more for you than where you currently are.

Your thermostat isn't permanent. It's adjustable. But you have to be intentional about adjusting it. Don't just work on your bank account—work on your internal setting. Because your external results will never consistently exceed your internal expectations.

Guarding Your Mind in a Negative World

Let me be honest with you: maintaining a wealth-building mindset in a world full of negativity is a daily battle. Social media is filled with comparison and materialism. The news cycle is dominated by economic doom and gloom. Even well-meaning friends and family can pour cold water on your dreams with their own fears and doubts.

So how do you protect your mindset when the world is constantly trying to pull it down?

First, be intentional about your morning routine. The first thirty minutes of your day set the tone for everything that follows. Before you check your phone, before you scroll social media, before you turn on the news—spend time in prayer, read Scripture, and declare God's promises over your life and finances. Fill your mind with truth before the world has a chance to fill it with lies.

Second, create a "vision board" or "faith file" that you review regularly. Include pictures of the properties you want to own, the lifestyle you're building toward, and the impact you want to make. Include Scripture verses about provision and blessing. Include your written goals and your family mission statement. When doubt creeps in, pull out that vision and let it remind you of where you're headed.

Third, practice gratitude daily. Write down three things you're thankful for every morning or every evening. Gratitude shifts your focus from what you lack to what you have—and that shift creates a mental environment where faith and abundance can flourish.

Fourth, limit your exposure to negativity. That doesn't mean burying your head in the sand. It means being selective about what you consume. Unfollow accounts that make you feel inadequate. Reduce time spent watching news that creates anxiety without providing actionable information. Replace negative inputs with educational content, inspiring stories, and the Word of God.

Your mind is the battlefield. If you win there, you win everywhere. Guard it fiercely.

CHAPTER 3

Faith Without Works Is Dead

"What good is it, my brothers and sisters, if someone claims to have faith but has no deeds?" — James 2:14

I love to pray. I mean it—I'm a firm believer in the power of prayer. I've seen God move mountains in response to prayer. I've seen doors open, deals close, and breakthroughs happen that only God could have orchestrated.

But here's something I've also learned the hard way: prayer without action is just wishful thinking.

I know that might ruffle some feathers, but hear me out. James 2:17 makes it plain: "Faith by itself, if it is not accompanied by action, is dead." That's not my opinion—that's the Word of God. And it applies to your finances just as much as it applies to every other area of your life.

I've met so many believers who are praying for financial breakthroughs but aren't doing anything to position themselves for one. They're praying for a better job but haven't updated their resume in five years. They're praying for a business but haven't written a business plan. They're praying for wealth but have never opened an investment account.

Don't get me wrong—I'm not minimizing prayer. Prayer is essential. But God responds to faith that moves. Think about it. When God parted the Red Sea, the Israelites still had to walk through it. When Joshua faced the walls of Jericho, he still had to march around them. When David faced Goliath, he still had to pick up the stone and sling it.

God provides the miracle, but He often requires the movement. And your financial life is no different.

The Action Gap

There's a gap that exists between where most people are and where they want to be. I call it the action gap. It's the space between knowing what to do and actually doing it. And it's where most dreams go to die.

Think about how many financial books, podcasts, and YouTube videos you've consumed. You probably know more about investing, budgeting, and wealth-building than ninety percent of the population. But has that knowledge translated into action? Have you opened that investment account? Have you started that budget? Have you looked into buying your first property?

If the answer is no, you're not alone. Most people get stuck in the learning phase because learning feels productive without the risk of failure. But learning without doing is just entertainment. It's financial Netflix. You feel like you're making progress, but your bank account tells a different story.

So what keeps people stuck in the action gap? Fear. Fear of making a mistake. Fear of losing money. Fear of looking foolish. Fear of stepping out and falling flat on your face.

And I get it. I've felt every single one of those fears. When I was looking at my first investment property, my hands were literally shaking. My mind was running through every possible worst-case scenario. What if the tenants don't pay? What if the roof caves in? What if I lose everything?

But then I heard that still, small voice in my spirit say, "Trust me." And I took the step. Was I scared? Absolutely. Did everything go perfectly? Not even close. But I took action, and that action changed the trajectory of my entire life.

Success doesn't happen by accident. It happens when you push past the fear and take the step. Even if it's a small step. Even if it's imperfect. Even if it's terrifying. Just move.

Practical Faith in Action

So what does practical faith look like when it comes to building wealth? Let me give you some examples.

Practical faith looks like setting up an automatic transfer to your savings account every payday, even if it's only twenty-five dollars. It looks like pulling your credit report and facing whatever's on it so you can start fixing it. It looks like driving to that neighborhood you've been curious about and looking at properties. It looks like having an honest conversation with your spouse about money, even when it's uncomfortable.

Practical faith looks like signing up for that real estate course. It looks like attending that networking event where you don't know anyone. It looks like calling that mortgage broker and asking questions, even if you feel like you're not ready. It looks like making an offer on a property when everything in your flesh is screaming to play it safe.

Each of these actions is a step of faith. And here's what's beautiful about faith: it doesn't have to be perfect. It just has to be real. God doesn't require you to have it all figured out. He just requires you to move.

Think about the woman in the Bible who had been bleeding for twelve years. She didn't have a perfect plan. She didn't have everything figured out. All she knew was that if she could just touch the hem of Jesus's garment, she would be healed. So she pushed through the crowd and reached out. And her faith made her whole.

Your financial healing might start the same way—with one imperfect, faith-filled reach toward something better.

I believe God honors imperfect action taken in faith far more than He honors perfect plans that never leave your notebook. So stop waiting for everything to line up. Stop waiting until you feel ready. Stop waiting for the "right time." The truth is, the perfect time to start is now.

Creating a Bias Toward Action

If you want to build wealth, you need to develop what I call a bias toward action. That means when you're faced with a decision, your default is to move rather than to wait. It means you'd rather make a mistake and learn from it than sit on the sidelines and never get in the game.

Now, I'm not saying be reckless. A bias toward action doesn't mean you skip due diligence or ignore wise counsel. It means that once you've done your research, sought advice, and prayed about it, you pull the trigger. You don't sit in analysis paralysis for six more months.

Here's a practical way to start building this muscle. Every single day, I want you to do one thing that moves you closer to your financial goals. Just one thing. It could be something small, like reading ten pages of a finance book. Or something bigger, like scheduling a meeting with a financial advisor. The size of the action doesn't matter as much as the consistency of the action.

Over time, these daily actions compound. They build momentum. They create habits. And before you know it, you've transformed from someone who talks about wealth to someone who's actually building it.

I often tell the people I mentor: don't wait until you have the whole staircase figured out. Just take the first step. God will illuminate the next step when you get there. That's how faith works. You step into the unknown, and He makes a way.

Hebrews 11:1 says, "Faith is confidence in what we hope for and assurance about what we do not see." You don't need to see the whole picture. You just need to trust the One who painted it.

So here's your challenge: before you go to bed tonight, take one action toward your financial future. Send one email. Make one phone call. Open one account. Write one goal down. Just do something.

Faith without works is dead. But faith with works? That's unstoppable. That's where miracles happen. That's where generational wealth begins.

Trust the process. Take the step. Watch God move.

The Compound Effect of Daily Action

Let me share a story that illustrates the power of daily action. One of my mentees—I'll call him Marcus—came to me completely overwhelmed. He wanted to invest in real estate, but he had bad credit, minimal savings, and no idea where to start. By the world's standards, he had no business thinking about real estate.

But Marcus had something most people don't: he was willing to do one thing every single day. For the first thirty days, his daily action was small. Day one, he pulled his credit report. Day two, he disputed an error. Day three, he set up automatic payments on his bills. Day four, he opened a high-yield savings account. Day five, he transferred twenty-five dollars into it. Day six, he read ten pages of a real estate book.

None of these actions were dramatic. None of them made for exciting social media posts. But they compounded. After six months, Marcus had raised his credit score by eighty points, saved two thousand dollars, and educated himself enough to start analyzing deals with confidence. After twelve months, he closed on his first property—a small duplex that cash-flowed three hundred dollars a month.

That's the compound effect of daily action. It's not about making one massive move. It's about making one small move, every single day, consistently over time. And that's how faith operates too—step by step, day by day, trusting God with each small act of obedience.

Don't despise small beginnings. Zechariah 4:10 asks, "Who dares despise the day of small things?" Those small things are the building blocks of your legacy. Embrace them. Be faithful in them. And watch them multiply into something you never imagined possible.

Reflection and Action Steps

Your assignment is simple but non-negotiable. Right now, write down seven actions you can take this week—one for each day—that move you closer to your financial goals. They don't have to be big. In fact, the smaller and more specific, the better.

Monday: Pull your credit report and review it for errors. Tuesday: Set up an automatic transfer of any amount to your savings account. Wednesday: Listen to one episode of a real estate or personal finance podcast. Thursday: Calculate your monthly expenses and identify one area where you can cut back. Friday: Research one investment opportunity—a REIT, a local investment group, or a rental property listing. Saturday: Read one chapter of a book about money or investing. Sunday: Pray over your financial goals and ask God for wisdom and direction.

At the end of the week, reflect on what you've accomplished. You'll be amazed at how much progress seven small actions can produce. Then do it again the next week. And the week after that. This is how legacies are built—one faithful action at a time.

When God Says Wait

I've talked a lot in this chapter about taking action, and I stand by every word. But I'd be dishonest if I didn't acknowledge that sometimes God says wait. And waiting is its own form of faith.

There have been seasons in my life when I was ready to move—ready to close a deal, ready to launch a project, ready to make a big financial leap—and God put the brakes on. Not because the opportunity was bad, but because the timing wasn't right. Maybe I wasn't ready. Maybe the market wasn't ready. Maybe there was something better around the corner that I couldn't see yet.

And in those seasons, waiting felt like torture. Every fiber of my being wanted to move, but God was saying, "Not yet."

Here's what I've learned about divine waiting: it's never wasted time. God uses waiting seasons to prepare you. He's building your character, deepening your faith, and positioning the pieces on the board for something you can't see yet. Isaiah 40:31 says, "Those who wait on the Lord shall renew their strength." Waiting on God isn't passive—it's an active posture of trust and preparation.

So how do you tell the difference between divine waiting and fear-based procrastination? Prayer and counsel. If you've prayed about a decision and consistently feel a check in your spirit, that might be God saying wait. If wise mentors are urging caution, listen. But if you're avoiding action simply because you're afraid, that's not God—that's fear. And fear is not a reliable advisor.

The key is to stay ready while you wait. Keep learning. Keep saving. Keep building relationships. So that when God says "Go," you can move immediately with confidence and preparation.

CHAPTER 4

Breaking Generational Curses

"No longer will they say, 'Parents have eaten sour grapes, and the children's teeth are set on edge.' Instead, everyone will die for their own sin." — Jeremiah 31:29–30

Let me tell you something that not enough people talk about: poverty is learned. It's not a genetic condition. It's not a curse from God. And it's definitely not your destiny. Poverty is a pattern—a pattern of thinking, a pattern of behavior, and a pattern of choices that gets passed down from one generation to the next.

And if nobody breaks the pattern, it just keeps repeating.

I grew up watching the adults around me live paycheck to paycheck. I watched them rob Peter to pay Paul. I watched them avoid the mail because they were afraid of what was inside the envelopes. I watched them argue about money at the kitchen table and pretend everything was fine in public.

Nobody taught me about investing. Nobody talked to me about credit scores. Nobody showed me how to build a budget. And I don't blame them—they didn't know because nobody taught them either. That's how generational cycles work. What you don't know, you can't teach. And what you can't teach, you pass down by default.

But here's the good news—and don't miss this—you can be the one who breaks the cycle. You can be the person in your family who says, "This stops with me." You can be the first to build real wealth, the first to own property, the first to leave an inheritance for your children's children.

And that's exactly what God is calling you to do.

Understanding the Roots

Before you can break a cycle, you have to understand where it started. And for most families, the cycle of financial struggle has deep roots.

Sometimes those roots are historical. Entire communities have been systematically denied access to banking, homeownership, education, and fair wages. That's not ancient history—the effects of those injustices are still being felt today. If your grandparents couldn't get a mortgage, they couldn't build equity. If they couldn't build equity, they couldn't leave an inheritance. And if they couldn't leave an inheritance, your parents started from zero. And so did you.

Sometimes the roots are cultural. Maybe your family came from a background where talking about money was considered rude or inappropriate. Maybe the prevailing attitude was "we don't talk about that" or "money is the root of all evil"—which, by the way, is a misquote. The verse actually says the love of money is the root of all kinds of evil. Money itself is neutral. It's a tool. And like any tool, it can be used for good or for harm.

Sometimes the roots are personal. Maybe your parents went through a bankruptcy, a foreclosure, or a financial scandal that left a mark on the whole family. Maybe they made bad decisions that created a ripple effect you're still dealing with today.

Whatever the roots, here's the important thing: understanding them doesn't mean being defined by them. You can acknowledge where you came from without being imprisoned by it. In fact, understanding your roots gives you power—because once you know what went wrong, you can intentionally choose a different path.

God is in the business of redemption. He takes broken things and makes them beautiful. He takes dead things and brings them back to life. And He can take a family history of financial struggle and turn it into a story of generational blessing.

But it starts with you making a decision. A decision to learn what wasn't taught. A decision to do what wasn't modeled. A decision to build what's never been built before in your family.

The Debts You Didn't Choose

One of the hardest things about generational financial cycles is dealing with the debts and burdens that aren't even yours. Maybe you're supporting aging parents who never saved for retirement. Maybe you're paying off student loans because nobody in your family could help with college. Maybe you're the "family ATM"—the one everyone calls when they need money.

If that's you, I want you to hear this: you can love your family and still set boundaries. You can honor your parents and still build your own financial future. You can be generous and still be wise.

I've had to learn this the hard way. There was a time in my life when I was giving money to family members every month—money I couldn't really afford to give. I was doing it out of love, but I was also doing it out of guilt. I felt like because I was doing better than everyone else, I was obligated to carry everyone. And you know what that led to? Resentment. Burnout. And a savings account that was practically empty.

It took a mentor sitting me down and saying, "You can't pour from an empty cup. If you bankrupt yourself trying to save everyone else, you won't be able to help anyone—including yourself."

That was a wake-up call. I realized that the most loving thing I could do for my family wasn't to hand them money every time they asked. It was to build something so strong, so stable, so lasting that it could bless them for generations. And that required me to make some hard decisions in the short term for the sake of the long term.

If you're in that position right now, give yourself grace. You don't have to fix everything overnight. But you do need to start being intentional about where your money goes and why. You need a plan. And we're going to build one together in the chapters ahead.

Writing a New Financial Story

Here's the truth: you are the author of the next chapter of your family's financial story. What happened before you was out of your control. But what happens from here? That's on you.

And I don't say that to put pressure on you. I say it to empower you. Because the fact that you're reading this book tells me something about you—you're not content with the status quo. You're not willing to let the patterns of the past dictate the possibilities of the future. You're ready for change.

So let's talk about what that change looks like practically. First, you need to get honest about where you are. That means pulling your credit report, adding up your debts, calculating your net worth, and looking at your spending habits without judgment. This is your starting line. You can't get where you're going if you don't know where you are.

Second, you need to cast a vision for where you're headed. What does financial freedom look like for you? Is it owning your first rental property? Having six months of expenses in savings? Retiring by a certain age? Leaving a million-dollar inheritance? Get specific. Write it down.

Habakkuk 2:2 says, "Write the vision; make it plain on tablets, so he may run who reads it." When the vision is clear, the path becomes clearer too.

Third, you need to commit to the process. Breaking generational cycles doesn't happen in a weekend. It takes years of consistent, faithful effort. There will be setbacks. There will be seasons where it feels like nothing is working. But trust the process. The seeds you plant today will produce a harvest your children and grandchildren will enjoy.

I want you to imagine something for a moment. Picture your grandchild, twenty or thirty years from now, standing in front of a home that your family owns—free and clear. Picture them starting a business with capital from a family trust that you established. Picture them going to college without a single dollar of debt because you set up an education fund. Picture them telling their friends, "My grandparent changed everything for our family."

That's the legacy you're building. That's the curse you're breaking. That's the story you're writing.

And it starts right here, right now, with you.

So what's your next move? Don't just sit on this—take action today. Pull that credit report. Open that savings account. Have that money conversation with your spouse. Do one thing that your future self will thank you for.

Remember, God rewards those who trust Him and take bold steps forward. You're not just changing your financial situation—you're changing your family tree.

This is your moment. Own it.

Forgiveness and Financial Freedom

There's an aspect of breaking generational curses that rarely gets talked about in finance books: forgiveness. You may be carrying bitterness, resentment, or anger toward the people who should have taught you about money but didn't. You may be frustrated with parents who made poor financial decisions that affected your life. You may be angry at a system that was stacked against your family from the start.

And those feelings are valid. I'm not going to tell you to just get over it. But I am going to tell you that holding onto that anger will keep you chained to the very cycle you're trying to break.

Unforgiveness is heavy. It takes up mental and emotional space that could be used for vision, creativity, and forward movement. When you're carrying bitterness, it colors every financial decision you make. It makes you reactive instead of proactive. It keeps you focused on what went wrong instead of what could go right.

Forgiveness doesn't mean what happened was okay. It doesn't mean you forget. It means you release the weight so you can run your race unhindered. Hebrews 12:1 tells us to "throw off everything that hinders and the sin that so easily entangles" so that we can "run with perseverance the race marked out for us."

If there's someone you need to forgive—a parent, a former partner, yourself—do it today. Not for their sake, but for yours. Because you cannot build a future of abundance on a foundation of bitterness. Let it go. Give it to God. And step into the freedom that's waiting for you on the other side.

The moment you release the past is the moment you become free to build the future. And that future? It's going to be something beautiful.

Reflection and Action Steps

This chapter's assignment is deeply personal, and I want you to approach it with honesty and grace.

First, write a letter—you don't have to send it—to the person or people who shaped your early relationship with money. It might be a parent, a guardian, or even yourself. Acknowledge what happened, express how it affected you, and then make a conscious decision to release it. This is between you and God.

Second, write your family's new financial mission statement. In one to three sentences, describe the financial legacy you are now building. Something like: "The [last name] family is committed to building wealth through faith, education, and wise stewardship. We break cycles of financial lack and create opportunities for every generation that follows." Put it somewhere you'll see it every day.

Third, pull your credit report if you haven't already. Sit with it. Study it. No judgment, no shame—just information. This is your starting point. Circle the items that need attention and make a plan to address the top three over the next sixty days.

You are not defined by what was. You are defined by what will be. And what will be starts with the decisions you make today.

The Power of Being First

There's something incredibly powerful about being the first person in your family to do something. The first to go to college. The first to own a business. The first to invest in real estate. The first to create a will or a trust.

Being first is lonely. There's no roadmap from your family. There's no one to call when things get confusing. There's no one who really understands the pressure you're under or the decisions you're facing.

But being first is also revolutionary. Because when you break through, you create a path that didn't exist before. Your children won't be first—they'll be second. And your grandchildren will be third. Each generation that follows you will start further ahead, with more resources, more knowledge, and more support than you had.

That's the beauty of being a cycle-breaker. The struggle is real, but the impact is generational. You're not just building for yourself—you're building for people who will never know the poverty, the lack, or the limitation that you knew. And that is worth every sacrifice, every late night, and every uncomfortable step of faith.

Moses led the Israelites out of Egypt, but he never entered the Promised Land himself. Joshua did. But Joshua couldn't have entered without Moses's leadership and sacrifice. You might be the Moses of your family—the one who endures the wilderness so that the next generation can enter the land of promise.

That's not a burden. That's an honor. Carry it with pride. Carry it with faith. And know that what you're building matters more than you'll ever fully see.

CHAPTER 5

Your First Assignment: Get Financially Literate

"The wise store up choice food and olive oil, but fools gulp theirs down." — Proverbs 21:20

If I could go back in time and give my younger self one piece of advice, it would be this: learn about money before you try to make money. Because making money without understanding money is like filling a bucket with holes in it. No matter how much you pour in, it keeps draining out.

Financial literacy is the foundation that everything else in this book is built on. You can't invest wisely if you don't understand how investing works. You can't build wealth if you don't know the difference between an asset and a liability. You can't protect your legacy if you've never heard of an LLC or a living trust.

And here's what frustrates me: this stuff should have been taught in school. We spent years learning algebra and chemistry, but nobody taught us how to balance a checkbook, read a mortgage statement, or file taxes. The system was not designed to make you financially free—it was designed to make you a good employee. And there's nothing wrong with being an employee, but you need to know that employment alone will never make you wealthy.

The good news is that it's never too late to learn. Whether you're eighteen or sixty-eight, you can start building your financial knowledge today. And that's exactly what this chapter is about. I'm going to walk you through the fundamentals—the stuff you absolutely need to know to start building wealth with confidence.

Budgeting: Know Where Your Money Goes

Let's start with the basics. Do you know where your money goes every month? And I don't mean a general idea—I mean specifically. Can you tell me, down to the dollar, how much you spent on food last month? On subscriptions? On impulse purchases?

If you can't, you're not alone. Studies consistently show that most Americans have no idea where their money goes. And that's a problem, because you can't manage what you don't measure.

A budget isn't a punishment. I need you to hear that. A budget isn't about restricting your life—it's about directing your life. It's about telling your money where to go instead of wondering where it went. A budget gives you control. It gives you clarity. And it gives you the power to make intentional choices about your financial future.

Here's a simple framework to get you started. Take your total monthly income after taxes. Then allocate it into three categories: needs, wants, and wealth-building. Your needs include housing, utilities, transportation, food, and insurance—the essentials you can't live without. Aim to keep this at about fifty percent of your income. Your wants include dining out, entertainment, shopping, and hobbies—the things that make life enjoyable but aren't essential. Aim for about thirty percent. Your wealth-building category includes savings, investments, debt payoff, and giving—the things that move you toward your long-term goals. Aim for at least twenty percent, and increase this number as your income grows.

Is this the only way to budget? No. There are tons of methods out there. But the specific method matters less than the discipline of doing it. Find a system that works for you and stick with it. Review it monthly. Adjust as needed. And remember: a budget is a living document, not a one-time exercise.

I'll be honest with you—I didn't start budgeting until I was in my mid-twenties, and I wish I'd started sooner. The moment I started tracking my spending, I found hundreds of dollars a month that were slipping through the cracks—subscriptions I forgot about, meals I didn't need, and purchases I made out of boredom.

When you see where your money is really going, it changes everything. You stop feeling broke and start feeling empowered. Because now you're in control.

Credit: Your Financial Reputation

Let's talk about credit. Your credit score is essentially your financial reputation. It tells lenders, landlords, and even some employers how reliable you are with money. And whether you like it or not, it has a massive impact on your ability to build wealth.

A good credit score can save you tens of thousands of dollars over your lifetime. It gets you lower interest rates on mortgages, better terms on business loans, and access to opportunities that aren't available to people with poor credit. A bad credit score? It costs you money every single day in the form of higher rates, denied applications, and missed opportunities.

So where do you stand? If you don't know your credit score, that's your first assignment. Go to a free credit monitoring service and pull your score today. Don't be afraid of what you see. Remember, this is your starting line, not your finish line.

If your score needs work, here are the fundamentals. Pay your bills on time—every single time. Payment history is the single biggest factor in your credit score. Keep your credit card balances low—ideally below thirty percent of your available credit. Don't close old credit accounts, because the length of your credit history matters. And check your credit report regularly for errors, because mistakes happen more often than you'd think.

If your credit is in rough shape, don't despair. I've seen people go from the 400s to the 700s in under two years with consistent effort. It's not about where you start—it's about the direction you're heading. Every on-time payment is a step forward. Every balance you pay down is a step forward. Every responsible financial decision you make is a step forward.

And here's a faith perspective on credit: think of it as stewardship of your reputation. Proverbs 22:1 says, "A good name is more desirable than great riches." Your credit score is your financial name. Guard it. Build it. Treat it as the valuable asset it is.

Saving: Building Your Safety Net

Before you invest a single dollar, you need a financial safety net. I call it your "peace of mind fund." This is three to six months of living expenses set aside in an easily accessible savings account that you do not touch unless there's a genuine emergency.

Why is this so important? Because life happens. Cars break down. Medical bills show up. Jobs get eliminated. And if you don't have a financial cushion, one unexpected event can derail everything you've been building.

I've seen it happen too many times. Someone starts investing, starts building momentum, and then their transmission goes out. They don't have an emergency fund, so they're forced to sell their investments at a loss or rack up credit card debt to cover the repair. All that progress, gone.

Your emergency fund is your financial foundation. It's what allows you to take risks with confidence because you know you have a backup plan. It's what keeps you from making panic decisions when life throws a curveball.

If you're starting from zero, don't let the goal of three to six months overwhelm you. Start with a goal of one thousand dollars. Then work your way up. Automate the savings so it happens without you having to think about it. Even fifty dollars a paycheck adds up. And once that emergency fund is in place, you'll feel a weight lift off your shoulders that you didn't even know was there.

Debt: The Wealth Killer

Now let's address the elephant in the room: debt. Consumer debt—credit cards, car loans, personal loans, and student loans used for lifestyle spending—is one of the biggest obstacles to building wealth. It's a chain around your ankle that gets heavier with every passing month.

Here's a stat that should make you sit up straight: the average American household carries over six thousand dollars in credit card debt, often at interest rates of twenty percent or more. That means for every hundred dollars you owe, you're paying twenty dollars a year just for the privilege of owing it. That's money that could be invested, saved, or used to build your future.

Now, not all debt is bad. There's a difference between consumer debt and strategic debt. A mortgage on a rental property that produces cash flow every month? That's strategic debt. A business loan that helps you scale a profitable business? That's strategic debt. But a credit card balance from a shopping spree? That's wealth destruction in slow motion.

If you're carrying consumer debt, I want you to make a plan to eliminate it. List out all your debts from smallest to largest. Start attacking the smallest one while making minimum payments on the rest. Once the smallest is paid off, take that payment and add it to the next one. This is called the snowball method, and it works because it builds momentum and gives you quick wins that keep you motivated.

As you're paying off debt, stop creating new debt. Cut up the credit cards if you have to. Delete the shopping apps. Unsubscribe from the marketing emails. Do whatever it takes to stop the bleeding so you can start the healing.

And here's the spiritual side of debt: Proverbs 22:7 says, "The borrower is slave to the lender." God doesn't want you in bondage. He wants you free. Free to give. Free to invest. Free to build. And getting out of consumer debt is one of the most liberating things you'll ever do.

Stewardship: The Master Key

Everything I've talked about in this chapter—budgeting, credit, saving, and debt elimination—comes back to one word: stewardship. Stewardship is the practice of managing what God has given you with wisdom, faithfulness, and intentionality.

In the parable of the talents in Matthew 25, Jesus tells the story of a master who entrusts his servants with different amounts of money before going on a journey. Two of the servants invest wisely and multiply what they were given. The third buries his talent in the ground out of fear. When the master returns, he rewards the faithful stewards and rebukes the one who did nothing.

That story isn't just about money—it's about responsibility. God has given you resources—time, talent, and treasure. And He expects you to manage them well. Not perfectly, but faithfully. He's not looking for perfection—He's looking for faithfulness.

When you budget wisely, you're being a good steward. When you build your credit, you're being a good steward. When you save for emergencies, you're being a good steward. When you pay off debt, you're being a good steward. And when you take what you've learned and teach it to your children, you're being a generational steward.

So here's the bottom line: financial literacy is not optional. It's the price of admission to the wealth-building game. And if you've been sitting on the sidelines because you felt like you didn't know enough, let this chapter be your starting line.

You don't need a finance degree. You don't need to be a math genius. You just need a willing heart, a teachable spirit, and the discipline to apply what you learn.

If you take nothing else away from this chapter, take this: manage what you have, and God will trust you with more. That's not just a nice saying—it's a biblical principle. Luke 16:10 says, "Whoever can be trusted with very little can also be trusted with much."

Start where you are. Use what you have. Do what you can. And watch God multiply the rest. Because every dollar you save, every debt you eliminate, and every point you add to your credit score is bringing you one step closer to owning your first investment property—and stepping into the promise of land that God established in Genesis.

The perfect time to start is now. Don't wait. Your legacy is depending on it.

Reflection and Action Steps

This chapter was heavy on information, so your action steps are about implementation.

First, if you don't have a budget, create one this week. Use any method that works for you—a spreadsheet, an app, a notebook. Track every dollar for the next thirty days. At the end of the month, review where your money went and make adjustments.

Second, check your credit score using a free service. Write down the number and the date. This is your baseline. Set a goal for where you want it to be in six months and twelve months.

Third, if you don't have an emergency fund, open a separate savings account today and set up an automatic transfer. Even if it's ten dollars a week, start. The habit matters more than the amount.

Fourth, list all of your consumer debts from smallest to largest. Commit to paying off the smallest one first while making minimum payments on the rest. Once it's paid off, roll that payment to the next one.

Fifth, commit to your ongoing financial education. Choose one book, one podcast, or one course about personal finance or investing and start it this week. Never stop learning. The more you know, the more confident your financial decisions become.

Remember, financial literacy is a journey, not a destination. You don't have to master everything at once. But you do have to start. And starting is what separates the dreamers from the builders.

You're a builder. Now go prove it.

Resources for Continued Learning

Financial literacy is a lifelong journey, and I want to make sure you have the tools to continue growing long after you finish this book.

For books, I recommend starting with foundational texts on personal finance and investing. Look for authors who combine practical wisdom with real-world experience. Read books about real estate investing, personal money management, and entrepreneurship. Visit your local library—most of these books are available for free.

For podcasts, there are dozens of excellent shows dedicated to real estate, personal finance, and wealth-building. Listen during your commute, your workout, or while doing chores. Fifteen minutes a day of financial education adds up to over ninety hours a year—that's the equivalent of a college course.

For community, find a local real estate investment club, a business networking group, or a church-based financial ministry. Online communities can also be valuable—look for groups that are active, positive, and focused on education rather than hype.

For professional guidance, consider working with a fee-only financial advisor, a CPA who specializes in real estate or small business, and an estate planning attorney. These professionals pay for themselves many times over through the money they save you and the mistakes they help you avoid.

And never stop reading the Word of God for financial wisdom. The Bible contains more practical financial advice than most people realize—from the principles of saving in Proverbs to the investment strategies in Ecclesiastes to the stewardship teachings of Jesus. God's Word is the ultimate financial guide, and it will never steer you wrong.

Commit to being a lifelong learner. The day you stop learning is the day you stop growing. And an heir who stops growing eventually stops building.

Understanding Assets vs. Liabilities

One of the most important concepts in financial literacy—and one that surprisingly few people understand—is the difference between an asset and a liability.

An asset is something that puts money in your pocket. A rental property that generates monthly income is an asset. A dividend-paying stock is an asset. A business that produces profit is an asset. An asset works for you.

A liability is something that takes money out of your pocket. A car payment is a liability. A credit card balance is a liability. A subscription you barely use is a liability. Liabilities work against you.

Here's where it gets tricky: many things that people think are assets are actually liabilities. Your personal home, for example. Most people consider their house their biggest asset. But if it's not generating income and it costs you money every month in mortgage payments, taxes, insurance, and maintenance, it's technically a liability. It's a place to live—and that has value—but it's not putting money in your pocket.

I'm not saying don't buy a home. I'm saying understand the difference. Wealthy people focus on acquiring assets—things that generate income and grow in value. They use their income to buy assets first, and then they use the income from those assets to fund their lifestyle. Poor and middle-class people do the opposite—they use their income to fund their lifestyle first, and whatever's left (usually nothing) goes toward assets.

This one shift in thinking—prioritizing asset acquisition over lifestyle spending—can transform your financial trajectory within a few years. Start asking yourself before every major purchase: is this an asset or a liability? Does it put money in my pocket or take money out? The answer to that question should drive every financial decision you make.

This is exactly why real estate is at the heart of The HEIRS™ framework. A rental property that puts money in your pocket every month is the definition of an asset. And unlike stocks or other investments, real estate gives you something you can see, touch, and pass down to your children—just like the land God promised to Abraham and his seed.

When you understand and apply the asset-liability distinction, you'll start making fundamentally different choices about how you use your money. And those different choices lead to radically different outcomes.

PART TWO: STRATEGY — BUILDING THE KINGDOM

CHAPTER 6

Real Estate: The Promised Land of Wealth

"The earth is the Lord's, and everything in it, the world, and all who live in it." — Psalm 24:1

If you've been following my journey for any length of time, you know that real estate is my passion. Not because it's trendy. Not because it looks good on social media. But because I have personally seen real estate transform lives—my own included—in ways that no other investment can.

I stumbled into my first real estate deal at just twenty years old. I didn't have a pile of cash. I didn't have perfect credit. What I had was curiosity, a willingness to learn, and a God who kept placing the right people and opportunities in my path at exactly the right time.

That first deal was terrifying. I second-guessed myself a hundred times. I almost backed out more than once. But I took the step, closed the deal, and watched something amazing happen: the property started putting money in my pocket every single month. Not a lot at first—but enough to show me that this was real. This worked. And if I could do it once, I could do it again.

That one decision changed everything for me. And I believe it can change everything for you too.

Here's what you need to know about real estate: it is the single most proven wealth-building vehicle in history. More millionaires have been created through real estate than through any other investment. Period. And it's not hard to see why.

Why Real Estate Builds Wealth Like Nothing Else

Real estate builds wealth through four powerful mechanisms, and when you understand all four, you'll see why I'm so passionate about this.

The first is cash flow. When you own a rental property, tenants pay you rent every month. After you pay your mortgage, taxes, insurance, and maintenance, what's left over is cash flow—money in your pocket. This is passive income. It's money that comes in whether you go to work or not. And as you acquire more properties, that cash flow multiplies.

The second is appreciation. Over time, real estate tends to go up in value. A property you buy today for two hundred thousand dollars might be worth three hundred thousand in ten years. That's a hundred thousand dollars in wealth that was created while you slept. You didn't have to do anything extra—the market did the heavy lifting.

The third is equity buildup through mortgage paydown. Every month, when your tenant pays rent and that rent covers your mortgage, a portion of that payment goes toward paying down your loan balance. Your tenant is essentially buying the property for you. Think about that. Someone else is paying off your asset.

The fourth is tax advantages. Real estate offers some of the best tax benefits in the entire tax code. You can deduct mortgage interest, property taxes, repairs, and depreciation. You can do a 1031 exchange to defer capital gains when you sell. And in many cases, you can earn significant rental income while paying very little in taxes because of these deductions.

When you combine all four of these mechanisms—cash flow, appreciation, equity buildup, and tax advantages—you've got a wealth-building machine that's nearly impossible to beat. No stock, no cryptocurrency, no side hustle offers all four of these benefits simultaneously.

And here's the faith connection: land has always been central to God's promises. When God made a covenant with Abraham, what did He promise? Land. When He delivered the Israelites from Egypt, where did He take them? To the Promised Land—a land flowing with milk and honey. Throughout Scripture, land represents provision, inheritance, and generational blessing.

When you invest in real estate, you're not just making a financial move—you're stepping into a biblical principle that has been operating since the beginning of time.

Types of Real Estate Investing

One of the beautiful things about real estate is that there's not just one way to do it. There are many strategies, and you can choose the one that best fits your situation, your budget, and your goals.

Single-family rentals are the most common starting point for new investors. You buy a house, you rent it to a tenant, and you collect rent every month. It's simple, it's straightforward, and it works. This is where I started, and it's where I recommend most beginners start too.

Multi-family properties—duplexes, triplexes, and fourplexes—are another great option. With a multi-family, you get multiple streams of rent from a single property. And here's a powerful strategy called house hacking: you buy a duplex, live in one unit, and rent out the other. The rent from your tenant covers most or all of your mortgage. You're essentially living for free while building equity.

Fix-and-flip is for investors who want faster returns. You buy a distressed property at a discount, renovate it, and sell it for a profit. This strategy requires more hands-on work and carries more risk, but the returns can be significant. This is not where I'd suggest a beginner start, but it's a powerful tool once you've gained experience and built a team.

Wholesale real estate involves finding deeply discounted properties and selling the contract to another investor for a fee. You don't need money or credit to wholesale—you just need hustle and the ability to find deals. It's a great way to get started in real estate with very little capital.

Real estate investment trusts, or REITs, allow you to invest in real estate without actually buying property. A REIT is like a mutual fund for real estate—you buy shares of a company that owns income-producing properties. This is a good option if you want real estate exposure but aren't ready to buy property yet.

The point is this: there's an entry point for everyone. Whether you have a hundred dollars or a hundred thousand dollars, there's a way for you to get started in real estate. Don't let the lie that you need to be rich to invest keep you on the sidelines.

Getting Started: Your Real Estate Action Plan

Alright, so you're interested in real estate. Now what? Here's your action plan.

Start by getting educated. Read books about real estate investing. Listen to podcasts. Watch videos. Attend local real estate investment meetings. The more you learn, the more confident you'll feel when it's time to make a move. Some of the best resources out there are free—you just have to be intentional about seeking them out.

Next, get your finances in order. Pull your credit report and start working on your score if needed. Save for a down payment. Get pre-approved for a mortgage so you know what you can afford. Having your financial house in order before you start looking at properties gives you a massive advantage.

Then start analyzing deals. Learn how to run the numbers on a property. What's the purchase price? What will the rent be? What are the expenses—mortgage, taxes, insurance, maintenance, property management? What's the cash flow after all expenses? You need to be comfortable with these calculations before you make an offer.

Build your team. Real estate investing is not a solo sport. You need a real estate agent who understands investment properties. You need a lender who works with investors. You need a good inspector, a reliable contractor, and eventually a property manager. Start building these relationships now, even if you're not ready to buy yet.

And finally, take the leap. At some point, the research phase has to end and the action phase has to begin. You will never feel one hundred percent ready. There will always be another book to read, another video to watch, another question to ask. But there comes a point where you just have to make an offer, close a deal, and step into your future.

I'll never forget the day I closed on my first property. My hands were sweating, my heart was racing, and a voice in my head was telling me I was crazy. But a louder voice—God's voice—was telling me to trust Him. And when I signed those papers, something shifted. I went from being a person who talked about real estate to a person who owned real estate. And there is no feeling in the world like that.

Your deal is out there. Your property is out there. Your breakthrough is out there. You just have to go get it.

The perfect time to start is now. Trust God, trust the process, and take the step. Don't miss this opportunity. Your future self will thank you.

Common Fears About Real Estate (And Why They Shouldn't Stop You)

Let me address some of the fears I hear most often from people who are interested in real estate but haven't taken the leap yet.

"What if I buy a bad property?" This is why you do your due diligence. You run the numbers, get the property inspected, research the neighborhood, and consult with experienced investors. Bad deals happen when people skip these steps, not when they follow them. And even if you make a mistake on your first deal, the education you gain is worth more than the money you might lose.

"What if my tenants don't pay?" This is a real risk, but it's manageable. Screen your tenants thoroughly—check credit, verify income, call references. A good property management company can handle this for you. And even in the worst case, you can evict a non-paying tenant and find a new one. It's a setback, not a death sentence.

"What if the market crashes?" Real estate markets go up and down, just like stock markets. But here's the difference: people always need a place to live. Even during the 2008 financial crisis—the worst real estate downturn in modern history—landlords who bought wisely and held their properties came out fine. If your property produces positive cash flow, a temporary decline in market value doesn't affect your monthly income. You only lose money in a crash if you're forced to sell.

"I don't have enough money." As we'll discuss in Chapter 9, there are numerous ways to invest in real estate with little or no money down. House hacking, partnerships, seller financing, and other creative strategies make real estate accessible to people at virtually every income level.

Every one of these fears is legitimate. But none of them are disqualifying. Successful investors don't operate without fear—they operate despite fear. They acknowledge the risk, prepare for it, and move forward in faith.

Second Timothy 1:7 says, "God has not given us a spirit of fear, but of power, love, and a sound mind." Power to take action. Love that motivates you to build for your family. And a sound mind to make wise decisions. That's everything you need.

Reflection and Action Steps

Here's your assignment for this chapter. First, write down every fear or objection you have about real estate investing. Get them all out of your head and onto paper. Then next to each one, write a practical step you can take to address it. Fear of bad deals? Take a course on property analysis. Fear of tenants? Research tenant screening services. Fear of the unknown? Attend a local real estate investment group meeting this month.

Second, drive through three neighborhoods in your area that you think could be good investment markets. Look at the condition of the homes, the level of activity, and whether there are signs of growth or decline. This is how investors start to develop an eye for opportunity.

Third, look up three rental listings in your area and practice running the numbers. Calculate potential rent, estimate expenses, and determine the cash flow. You don't need to buy anything—just practice the analysis so it becomes second nature.

Real estate is not reserved for the elite. It's available to anyone with the courage to learn and the faith to act. Start building your knowledge now, and when the right deal comes along, you'll be ready.

My Biggest Real Estate Lesson

Let me share a story I don't tell very often. Early in my investing career, I fell in love with a property. It was a beautiful three-bedroom in a neighborhood I'd always admired. The kitchen was updated, the yard was big, and I could already picture tenants lining up to rent it.

There was just one problem: the numbers didn't work. The asking price was too high, the rents in the area were too low, and after expenses, I would have been losing money every month. But I wanted it. I let my emotions override my analysis. I convinced myself the market would go up, that I could charge higher rent, that it would all work out.

So I bought it. And for the first two years, I lost money every single month. I was subsidizing my investment out of my own pocket. It was stressful, it was frustrating, and it was entirely avoidable.

Eventually, the market did improve, and I was able to raise rents to a break-even point. But I spent two years learning a lesson I could have learned by simply sticking to my criteria: never let emotion override the numbers.

I share this not to scare you but to prepare you. Real estate investing is incredibly powerful, but it requires discipline. The properties that make you the most money are rarely the prettiest or the most exciting. They're the ones where the math works. They're the ones in the neighborhoods nobody's talking about yet. They're the ones that might not look like much today but will generate wealth for decades.

Fall in love with the numbers, not the property. That single piece of advice will save you more money than anything else I can teach you.

The Long Game: Why Patience Wins in Real Estate

In a world of instant gratification, real estate requires something that's increasingly rare: patience. And I'll be the first to admit—patience is not my natural strength. When I started investing, I wanted results immediately. I wanted every property to cash-flow from day one. I wanted appreciation to happen overnight. I wanted the wealth-building process to match the speed of my ambition.

But real estate doesn't work that way. Real estate is a long game. The wealth is built over years and decades, not weeks and months. And the investors who understand this are the ones who build the biggest portfolios and the most lasting wealth.

Here's why patience wins in real estate. First, rents increase over time. A property that cash-flows modestly today might cash-flow significantly in ten years as rents rise. The market rewards those who hold. Second, mortgage balances decrease over time. Every month that passes, your tenant is paying down your loan. After fifteen or thirty years, you own the property free and clear—generating pure profit. Third, appreciation compounds. A property that increases in value by just three or four percent per year will double in value within twenty years. And you didn't have to do anything extra—time did the work.

When you combine increasing rents, decreasing debt, and compounding appreciation, the wealth created over a twenty-to-thirty-year period is staggering. A single property purchased today for two hundred thousand dollars could be worth over four hundred thousand in twenty years, generating fifteen hundred dollars a month in rent with no mortgage payment. That's the power of the long game.

So don't get discouraged if your first property doesn't make you rich overnight. It's not supposed to. It's the first brick in a foundation that will support your family for generations. Keep adding bricks. Keep holding. Keep trusting the process.

Psalm 37:7 says, "Be still before the Lord and wait patiently for him." That's good life advice—and it's great real estate advice too. Play the long game. The harvest is coming.

CHAPTER 7

Your First Deal

"The plans of the diligent lead to profit as surely as haste leads to poverty." — Proverbs 21:5

Alright, let's get practical. In the last chapter, we talked about why real estate is such a powerful wealth-building tool. Now I want to walk you through, step by step, how to actually close your first deal. Because I know for a lot of you, the idea of buying an investment property feels overwhelming. There are so many moving pieces, so many numbers to crunch, and so many decisions to make.

But here's what I want you to remember: thousands of ordinary people close real estate deals every single day. People with less experience than you. People with less education than you. People with less money than you. If they can do it, so can you.

Your first deal will not be perfect. Let me say that again: your first deal will not be perfect. And that's okay. The goal of your first deal is not to hit a home run. The goal is to get in the game, learn the process, and build a foundation that you can scale from. Some of the most successful real estate investors I know will tell you that their first deal was messy, scary, and far from ideal. But it was that first deal that gave them the experience, confidence, and momentum to do the second, the third, and the thirtieth.

So let's break this down step by step.

Step One: Define Your Strategy and Market

The first thing you need to decide is what type of real estate investing you're going to pursue and where. Are you going to buy a single-family rental? A duplex to house hack? A wholesale deal? Each strategy has different requirements, different risk profiles, and different returns.

For most first-time investors, I recommend starting with a single-family rental or a small multi-family property in your local market. Why local? Because you know the area. You know which neighborhoods are up and coming. You know where people want to live. And you can physically visit the property whenever you need to. As you gain experience, you can expand to other markets. But for your first deal, keep it close to home.

Once you've chosen your strategy, you need to define your criteria. What price range are you looking in? What minimum cash flow do you need per month? What condition are you willing to buy in—turnkey, light renovation, or full rehab? Having clear criteria before you start looking at properties will save you time and prevent emotional decision-making.

I've seen too many new investors fall in love with a property because it has a nice kitchen or a big backyard, only to realize later that the numbers don't work. Your criteria should be based on numbers, not emotions. Remember, you're not buying a home—you're buying an investment. The property doesn't need to be a place you'd want to live—it needs to be a place that produces income.

Step Two: Get Your Financing in Order

Before you start shopping for properties, you need to know how you're going to pay for one. Most first-time investors use a mortgage, and there are several types available to you.

A conventional loan typically requires a down payment of fifteen to twenty-five percent for investment properties. The better your credit score, the better your interest rate will be. If you're house hacking—living in one unit of a multi-family property—you may qualify for an FHA loan, which requires as little as three and a half percent down. That's a game-changer for people who don't have a lot of cash saved up.

There are also portfolio lenders, hard money lenders, and private money lenders. Portfolio lenders are local banks that keep loans on their own books and may have more flexible qualification criteria. Hard money lenders provide short-term loans based on the property's value rather than your personal financial situation—these are often used for fix-and-flip deals. Private money comes from individuals—friends, family, or other investors who are willing to lend you money at an agreed-upon interest rate.

Whichever route you choose, the key is to get pre-approved before you start making offers. A pre-approval letter tells sellers that you're a serious buyer with the financial backing to close the deal. In a competitive market, this can be the difference between getting the property and losing it to another buyer.

And let me say this: don't let your current financial situation discourage you. I've seen people get creative with financing in ways that blow my mind. Partnerships, seller financing, lease options, subject-to deals—there are so many ways to structure a real estate transaction. Where there's a will and a way, God will make a way.

Step Three: Find and Analyze the Deal

Now comes the fun part: finding properties. You can search online through real estate listing sites, connect with wholesalers who have off-market deals, drive through neighborhoods looking for vacant or distressed properties, attend foreclosure auctions, or network with real estate agents who specialize in investment properties.

Once you find a property that looks promising, you need to analyze the numbers. And this is where most people either get paralyzed or skip steps. Neither is a good option. You need to be thorough but decisive.

Here's a simplified way to analyze a rental property. Start with the expected monthly rent. You can estimate this by looking at comparable rentals in the same area. Then subtract your monthly expenses: mortgage payment, property taxes, insurance, maintenance (budget about ten percent of rent), vacancy (budget about five to eight percent), and property management (about eight to ten percent of rent even if you plan to manage it yourself—because you won't always want to).

What's left is your monthly cash flow. For your first deal, aim for at least one hundred to two hundred dollars per month in positive cash flow after all expenses. It might not sound like a lot, but remember—you're also building equity, getting appreciation, and benefiting from tax deductions. The cash flow is just one piece of the wealth-building puzzle.

Run the numbers conservatively. Assume the worst-case scenario. If the deal still works with conservative estimates, it's probably a solid investment. If it only works with optimistic projections, walk away. There will always be another deal.

I cannot stress this enough: let the numbers guide your decisions, not your emotions. The properties that make you the most money are rarely the prettiest. They're the ones where the math works.

Step Four: Make the Offer, Close the Deal

Once you've found a property where the numbers work, it's time to make an offer. This is where a lot of people freeze up. They second-guess themselves. They think, "Maybe I should wait" or "What if there's a better deal around the corner?"

Don't fall into that trap. Perfectionism is the enemy of progress. If the deal meets your criteria and the numbers work, make the offer.

Work with your real estate agent to write a competitive offer. Include contingencies that protect you—an inspection contingency so you can back out if there are major issues, and a financing contingency in case your loan falls through. These contingencies give you an exit ramp if something goes sideways.

Once your offer is accepted, you'll enter the due diligence period. Get the property inspected by a qualified professional. Review the title report to make sure there are no liens or legal issues. Confirm your financing and finalize the numbers one more time.

Then comes closing day. You'll sign a mountain of paperwork, hand over your down payment and closing costs, and walk out as the owner of an investment property. I remember my first closing like it was yesterday. My hand was shaking so badly I could barely sign the documents. But when it was done, I felt a sense of accomplishment that I'd never felt before. I had done it. I was a real estate investor.

And you're going to feel that same thing. The nervousness, the excitement, the weight of the decision, and then the incredible relief and pride that comes from knowing you took the step. You did the thing that most people just talk about.

After closing, your job shifts from deal-finder to asset manager. Find a great tenant, maintain the property, collect your rent, and start looking for your next deal. Because one property is the beginning—not the destination.

Your first deal is out there waiting for you. Go find it. God has already prepared the way. You just have to walk in it.

Reflection and Action Steps

Your first deal is closer than you think. Here's how to move toward it this week.

First, decide on your strategy. Are you going to buy a single-family rental, house hack a duplex, or start with wholesaling? Write it down and commit to learning everything you can about that specific strategy for the next thirty days.

Second, contact a mortgage broker or lender and get pre-approved—or at least find out what you need to do to become pre-approvable. Knowing your financing options gives you confidence and clarity.

Third, start building your team. Reach out to one real estate agent who works with investors, one inspector, and one lender. Even if you're not ready to buy yet, these relationships take time to develop and will be invaluable when you're ready to move.

Fourth, analyze at least five properties this week using the simple cash flow analysis method described in this chapter. Practice makes progress. The more deals you analyze, the faster you'll recognize a good one when it appears.

Remember, your first deal will not be perfect. And that's perfectly fine. What matters is that you get in the game. The education, the confidence, and the momentum you gain from your first deal will carry you into your second, your fifth, and your twentieth. Just start.

The Power of Your First Deal's Story

Here's something you might not expect me to say: one of the most valuable things about your first deal isn't the money. It's the story.

When you close your first real estate deal, you become someone with a story to tell. And that story has power. It inspires other people to take action. It gives you credibility when you're networking. It attracts partners, mentors, and opportunities. And it fundamentally changes how you see yourself.

Before my first deal, I was a person who wanted to invest in real estate. After my first deal, I was a real estate investor. That identity shift was worth more than any profit margin. Because once you've done it once, you know you can do it again.

I've seen this pattern hundreds of times with the people I mentor. The first deal is always the hardest. It takes the longest. It involves the most fear and uncertainty. But once it's done, something clicks. The second deal comes faster. The third deal is easier. By the fifth deal, they're operating with a confidence and competence that didn't exist before.

So don't just think of your first deal as a financial transaction. Think of it as a transformation. It's the moment you cross from spectator to participant. From dreamer to doer. From someone who talks about building wealth to someone who's actually doing it.

And document the journey. Take photos. Keep a journal. Save the closing documents. Because someday, you'll look back on that first deal and realize it was the moment everything changed. And you'll have a story that helps someone else take their first step too.

CHAPTER 8

Multiple Streams of Income

"Invest in seven ventures, yes, in eight; you do not know what disaster may come upon the land." — Ecclesiastes 11:2

If there's one principle that separates the wealthy from the middle class, it's this: wealthy people have multiple streams of income. They don't rely on a single paycheck from a single employer to fund their entire life. They've diversified their income so that if one stream dries up, the others keep flowing.

Think about it this way. If you have one job and that job disappears, you have zero income. But if you have a job, a rental property, a side business, and some dividend-paying investments, losing your job hurts but it doesn't destroy you. You still have money coming in. You still have options. You still have time to figure out your next move.

The Bible actually supports this idea directly. Ecclesiastes 11:2 says to invest in seven ventures—yes, in eight—because you don't know what trouble may come.

That's diversification. That's God telling you not to put all your eggs in one basket.

Now, I'm not saying you need to launch eight businesses tomorrow. What I am saying is that you should be actively working toward building additional streams of income beyond your primary job. And in this chapter, I'm going to show you how.

The Income Stream Categories

There are three main categories of income, and understanding the difference between them is crucial to building wealth.

Earned income is what most people are familiar with. It's the money you receive in exchange for your time and labor. Your job salary, hourly wages, freelance fees, and consulting income all fall into this category. Earned income is important—it's what pays the bills and funds your investments. But it has a ceiling. There are only so many hours in a day, and your earning potential is limited by how much time you can trade for money.

Portfolio income comes from investments—stocks, bonds, mutual funds, and capital gains from selling assets. When you buy shares of a company and that company's stock price goes up, the profit you make when you sell is portfolio income. When a stock pays you a dividend every quarter, that's portfolio income. This type of income requires money to make money, but it allows your wealth to grow without additional time investment.

Passive income is the holy grail of wealth-building. This is money that comes in with little to no ongoing effort. Rental income from real estate, royalties from a book or product, revenue from a digital course, income from a business that runs without you—these are all forms of passive income. Now, I'll be honest—nothing is truly passive in the beginning. It takes significant work upfront to build passive income streams. But once they're established, they can produce money for years or even decades with minimal maintenance.

Your goal should be to build income in all three categories. Use your earned income to fund investments that generate portfolio and passive income. Over time, as your passive income grows, you become less dependent on your earned income. That's the path to financial freedom. That's when you stop working because you have to and start working because you want to.

Building a Business: Your Kingdom Enterprise

One of the most powerful ways to create additional income—and eventually wealth—is to start a business. And before you say, "I'm not an entrepreneur," hear me out.

You don't have to launch a Fortune 500 company. You don't have to invent a new product. You don't even have to quit your day job—at least not right away. What you need is a skill, a service, or a solution that people are willing to pay for.

Think about what you're good at. Maybe you're great at organizing—you could start a professional organizing or event planning business. Maybe you're skilled at writing—you could freelance as a copywriter or content creator. Maybe you know how to fix things—you could start a handyman or property maintenance service. Maybe you have expertise in a specific area—you could create an online course or coaching program.

The beauty of entrepreneurship is that it gives you unlimited earning potential. There's no boss telling you what your labor is worth. There's no corporate ladder to climb. Your income is a direct reflection of the value you bring to the marketplace.

And here's where faith comes in. I believe God gives every person gifts, talents, and abilities that can be used not just to serve others but to generate wealth. When you build a business around your God-given gifts, you're operating in your purpose. You're creating value. You're solving problems. And you're being compensated for it.

The key is to start small, start lean, and start now. Don't wait until you have the perfect business plan, the perfect website, or the perfect logo. Those things can come later. What matters most is that you start serving, start solving problems, and start generating revenue.

Many of the wealthiest people I know started their businesses as side hustles. They worked their nine-to-five during the day and built their dream at night and on weekends. It wasn't glamorous. It wasn't easy. But over time, the side hustle outgrew the job. And that's when everything changed.

Digital Income and the Modern Opportunity

We live in one of the most incredible times in human history to build wealth. The internet has democratized opportunity in ways that previous generations could never have imagined. Today, you can reach customers around the world from your living room. You can sell products without holding inventory. You can teach thousands of people without being in a classroom.

Digital income streams include things like online courses, e-books, affiliate marketing, content creation on platforms like YouTube or podcasts, print-on-demand merchandise, software tools, and membership communities. These businesses often have low startup costs, high profit margins, and the potential for significant scale.

If you have knowledge or expertise in any area—real estate, cooking, fitness, parenting, photography, biblical teaching, personal finance—there are people out there who would pay to learn from you. The question is not whether there's a market for what you know. The question is whether you're willing to package it and put it out there.

I've seen people in my mentorship programs create digital products that now generate thousands of dollars a month in passive income. They did the work once—recorded the course, wrote the e-book, built the membership site—and now that product sells while they sleep.

That's the power of building in the digital space. And it pairs beautifully with real estate investing. Your job pays the bills, your digital business accelerates your savings, and your real estate portfolio builds long-term wealth. When all three are working together, you've got an engine that's hard to stop.

Here's the bottom line: the days of relying on a single income source are over. If you want to build generational wealth, you need multiple streams flowing into your financial life. Start with what you have, build from where you are, and trust God to multiply your efforts.

Success doesn't happen by accident. It happens when you position yourself with intention, strategy, and faith. You've got what it takes. Now go build it.

Protecting Your Income Streams

As you build multiple streams of income, it's important to protect them. Diversification isn't just about having multiple income sources—it's about making sure those sources are resilient.

For your earned income, invest in your skills continuously. The marketplace rewards people who are constantly growing, learning, and adapting. Make yourself indispensable at your job while simultaneously building your exit strategy.

For your business income, build systems that allow the business to operate without you being involved in every detail. Document your processes. Hire and train good people. Create standard operating procedures. A business that depends entirely on you is not a business—it's a job with extra headaches.

For your investment income, diversify across asset classes and strategies. Don't put all your money in one property, one stock, or one market. Spread your risk so that a downturn in one area doesn't wipe you out.

And for all your income streams, maintain good records, pay your taxes, and work with professionals—accountants, attorneys, and financial advisors—who can help you protect and optimize what you've built.

Remember, building wealth is a marathon, not a sprint. The goal isn't to get rich quick—it's to build sustainable, diversified income that provides for your family today and for generations to come. Take it step by step, stream by stream, and trust God with the growth.

Reflection and Action Steps

Time to take inventory. Write down every source of income you currently have. For most people, it's one—their job. That's okay. Now write down three additional income streams you could realistically start building in the next twelve months.

For each potential income stream, answer these questions: What skills or resources do I already have that apply? What would I need to learn? How much time can I dedicate to it weekly? What's a realistic first milestone?

Then pick one—just one—and take your first step toward building it this week. Sign up for a course. Register a business name. List your first product. Make your first sales call. The action doesn't have to be huge. It just has to be real.

You were not designed to depend on a single source of income. You were designed to create, to build, and to multiply. Go build your next stream.

The Side Hustle Mindset

Let me talk about something that's near and dear to my heart: the side hustle. A lot of people think of side hustles as something you do when you're desperate—driving for a rideshare, selling stuff online, freelancing on the weekends. And while there's nothing wrong with any of those things, I want to reframe how you think about side hustles.

A side hustle isn't a sign of desperation. It's a sign of ambition. It's a sign that you refuse to let your nine-to-five determine your financial ceiling. It's a sign that you're willing to sacrifice short-term comfort for long-term freedom.

The most successful people I know all had a side hustle phase. A period where they worked their job during the day and built their dream at night. They were tired. They missed social events. They sacrificed weekends. But they were building something that their job alone could never provide: an additional stream of income that they controlled.

Here's the key: your side hustle should be strategic, not random. It should align with your skills, your interests, and your long-term goals. If your goal is real estate, your side hustle might be property management or real estate photography—something that earns money while building relevant knowledge and connections. If your goal is entrepreneurship, your side hustle might be consulting or freelancing in your area of expertise.

And treat your side hustle like a real business from day one. Keep separate finances. Track your income and expenses. Set goals and measure progress. Because the habits you build in the side hustle phase are the same habits that will serve you when that side hustle becomes your main thing.

Don't despise the side hustle season. Embrace it. It's the proving ground where your work ethic, your creativity, and your faith are tested and strengthened. And when you look back on it years from now, you'll be grateful for every late night and early morning that got you where you are.

From Employee to Owner: The Mental Shift

There's a moment in every wealth-builder's journey when they realize that working for someone else will never make them wealthy. Not because employment is bad—it's not—but because employment has a ceiling. Your salary is determined by someone else. Your schedule is determined by someone else. Your job security is determined by someone else.

Ownership has no ceiling. When you own an asset—a business, a property, an investment—your income potential is unlimited. Your schedule is yours. And your security is built on a foundation that you control.

But the shift from employee to owner isn't just financial—it's mental. As an employee, you're trained to follow instructions, minimize risk, and exchange time for money. As an owner, you have to make decisions, embrace calculated risk, and create value that generates income independent of your time.

This mental shift doesn't happen overnight. And it doesn't require you to quit your job tomorrow. What it requires is a change in how you see yourself. You start seeing your job not as your career but as your funding source—the capital engine that fuels your investing and business-building activities. You start using your evenings and weekends to build ownership stakes rather than just consuming entertainment. You start thinking about problems not as annoyances but as business opportunities.

The most powerful word in the vocabulary of wealth is "ownership." When you own, you build equity. When you own, you build wealth that grows independent of your labor. When you own, you create something that can be passed to the next generation.

You don't have to choose between being an employee and being an owner. The smartest path for most people is to be both—using employment income to fund ownership pursuits until the ownership income exceeds the employment income. Then you have options. And options are what wealth is really all about.

CHAPTER 9

Leverage and Other People's Money

"Where there is no guidance, a people falls, but in an abundance of counselors there is safety." — Proverbs 11:14

One of the biggest myths about building wealth is that you need to have money to make money. And while having capital certainly helps, it's not the only way—or even the best way—to get started. The concept I want to introduce you to in this chapter might just change the entire trajectory of your financial journey. It's called leverage.

Leverage means using resources you don't own to create results you couldn't achieve on your own. In the financial world, that often means using other people's money—OPM—to fund your investments and grow your wealth.

Does that sound risky? Maybe. But here's the truth: every major corporation, every real estate developer, and every successful entrepreneur in history has used leverage. When a company issues bonds to fund an expansion, that's leverage. When a developer gets a bank loan to build an apartment complex, that's leverage. When an entrepreneur raises capital from investors, that's leverage.

The question isn't whether leverage is good or bad. The question is whether you're using it wisely. And that's what this chapter is all about.

The Power of OPM in Real Estate

Real estate is one of the few asset classes where using other people's money is not only accepted—it's expected. Think about it. When you buy a home with a mortgage, you're putting down maybe five to twenty percent and the bank is covering the rest. That's leverage. You're controlling a two-hundred-thousand-dollar asset with twenty or forty thousand dollars of your own money.

And here's where it gets powerful. Let's say you buy a property for two hundred thousand dollars with a twenty percent down payment of forty thousand. Over the next few years, the property appreciates to two hundred and fifty thousand. You've made fifty thousand dollars in equity, but you only invested forty thousand. That's a one hundred and twenty-five percent return on your actual investment—even though the property itself only went up twenty-five percent.

That's the magic of leverage. You're amplifying your returns by using the bank's money to control an asset. And while your tenant pays the mortgage, your equity grows month after month.

But leverage works both ways. If the property decreases in value, your losses are also amplified. That's why it's critical to buy wisely—in good locations, at the right price, with numbers that work even in a downturn. Never over-leverage yourself. Always leave room for the unexpected.

The best investors I know use leverage strategically, not recklessly. They borrow at favorable terms, buy assets that produce income, and let the tenants service the debt. It's a beautiful system when it's executed with wisdom and discipline.

Creative Financing Strategies

Beyond traditional bank loans, there are several creative financing strategies that can help you get into deals with little to no money out of pocket. These are strategies that experienced investors use all the time, and there's no reason you can't use them too.

Seller financing is when the property owner acts as the bank. Instead of getting a mortgage from a traditional lender, you negotiate terms directly with the seller. They carry the note, and you make payments to them instead of a bank. This can be incredibly flexible—you can negotiate the down payment, interest rate, and repayment schedule. It's a win-win because the seller gets steady income and you get into a deal without jumping through all the hoops of traditional lending.

Subject-to deals involve purchasing a property subject to the existing mortgage. The loan stays in the seller's name, but you take over the payments and ownership of the property. This allows you to acquire property without qualifying for a new loan. It's an advanced strategy that requires proper legal guidance, but it can be a game-changer when used correctly.

Partnerships are another form of leverage. Maybe you've got the deal-finding skills but not the capital. Or maybe you've got the capital but not the time. Partnering with someone who has what you lack allows both of you to benefit. One partner brings the money, the other brings the expertise or the deal, and you split the profits according to your agreement.

Private money lending is when individuals—often people in your network—lend you money for real estate deals. They earn a return on their investment, and you get the capital to close deals. Building relationships with private money lenders can give you access to fast, flexible capital that traditional banks simply can't match.

Each of these strategies has its own pros, cons, and legal considerations. I strongly recommend working with a real estate attorney and a financial advisor before pursuing creative financing. But don't let the complexity scare you off. Every strategy starts with education and builds with experience.

Leveraging Relationships and Knowledge

Money isn't the only form of leverage. In fact, I'd argue that two other forms of leverage are even more valuable: relationships and knowledge.

Relationships are the currency of success. The people you know, the network you build, and the community you surround yourself with can open doors that money alone can't. A mentor who's been where you want to go can save you years of mistakes. A partner with complementary skills can help you close deals you couldn't do alone. A community of like-minded believers can encourage you when times get tough and celebrate with you when you win.

Proverbs 13:20 says, "Walk with the wise and become wise, for a companion of fools suffers harm." Your circle matters. If you're surrounded by people who are building wealth, who are pursuing their purpose, and who are walking in faith, you'll be inspired to do the same. But if you're surrounded by people who complain about money, make excuses, and refuse to grow, that energy will drag you down.

Be intentional about who you spend your time with. Attend conferences, join investment groups, find a mentor, and build relationships with people who are where you want to be. These relationships will become some of the most valuable assets in your portfolio.

Knowledge is the other form of leverage that can't be taken from you. The more you learn about real estate, finance, business, and investing, the better decisions you'll make. And better decisions lead to better outcomes.

Invest in your education relentlessly. Read books. Take courses. Listen to podcasts. Attend workshops. The return on investment for education is infinite because the knowledge you gain compounds over your entire lifetime.

Here's the bottom line: you don't need to have it all figured out, and you don't need to have a fat bank account to start building wealth. You need leverage—financial leverage, relational leverage, and intellectual leverage. Use what you have, borrow what you don't, partner where it makes sense, and let God multiply the results.

I believe God honors those who step out in faith, use wisdom, and refuse to let excuses hold them back. You have more resources than you think. You have more connections than you realize. And you have a God who can do more with your little than you could ever do with a lot.

Trust the process. Take the step. And watch the doors open.

Reflection and Action Steps

Leverage can feel intimidating, so let's break this into manageable steps.

First, evaluate your current leverage position. Do you have a mortgage? A car loan? Business debt? Write it all down. For each debt, note the interest rate, the monthly payment, and whether it's consumer debt or strategic debt. This gives you clarity on where you stand.

Second, identify one relationship you can build this week that could open a door to leverage. Maybe it's a potential partner, a private money lender, a mentor, or a real estate agent who knows off-market deals. Send one message, make one call, attend one event. Relationship leverage starts with a single conversation.

Third, educate yourself on one creative financing strategy. Pick one from this chapter—seller financing, subject-to, partnerships, or private money—and spend this week learning everything you can about it. Read articles, watch videos, listen to podcasts. When an opportunity presents itself, you want to be ready with the knowledge to seize it.

Remember, leverage is not about being reckless. It's about being resourceful. God has placed resources around you—money, people, knowledge—that you may not even be aware of. Open your eyes, open your mind, and open yourself to the possibility that you can do more than you think with what you already have.

The Faith to Borrow Wisely

I want to address something that trips up a lot of Christians when it comes to leverage: the tension between borrowing and biblical principles.

You've probably heard Proverbs 22:7 quoted in the context of avoiding all debt: "The borrower is slave to the lender." And that verse is absolutely true when it comes to consumer debt—credit card balances, car loans on depreciating assets, and lifestyle debt that produces no return.

But I believe there's a difference between foolish borrowing and wise leveraging. When you borrow money to buy a liability—something that takes money out of your pocket—that's enslavement. But when you borrow money to acquire an asset—something that puts money in your pocket—that's stewardship.

Consider this: in the parable of the talents, the master didn't praise the servant who buried his money in the ground. He praised the servants who put their resources to work and produced a return. The one-talent servant played it safe, and the master called him wicked and lazy.

I'm not suggesting you go into reckless debt. What I am suggesting is that there's a faithful middle ground between burying your talent and being irresponsible. That middle ground is wise leverage—borrowing strategically, with clear math, clear risk assessment, and clear purpose.

Pray about every financial decision involving debt. Seek wise counsel. Run the numbers thoroughly. And if the deal makes sense, the risk is manageable, and God gives you peace, step forward in faith. Because sometimes the most faithful thing you can do is use the tools available to you—including other people's money—to build the kingdom and the legacy God has called you to create.

CHAPTER 10

Protecting What You Build

"A prudent person foresees danger and takes precautions. The simpleton goes blindly on and suffers the consequences." — Proverbs 27:12

There's a saying I love: "The best offense is a good defense." And when it comes to building generational wealth, that couldn't be more true. It's not enough to build wealth—you have to protect it. Because the same world that offers opportunity also presents risk. Lawsuits. Tax liabilities. Economic downturns. Unexpected events. If you're not prepared, one bad break can wipe out years of hard work.

This is the chapter that most wealth-building books skip, and it's one of the most important. Because what good is building a fortune if it can be taken from you? What good is owning ten properties if a single lawsuit can put them all at risk? What good is creating income if the tax man takes half of it?

Protection isn't sexy. It doesn't make for exciting Instagram posts. But it's the difference between building wealth that lasts one generation and building wealth that lasts four.

Legal Protection: LLCs and Business Entities

One of the first things you should do when you start investing in real estate or building a business is set up a legal entity. For most small investors and business owners, the most common choice is a Limited Liability Company, or LLC.

An LLC creates a legal separation between your personal assets and your business or investment assets. If someone slips and falls at your rental property and sues, they can go after the assets inside the LLC—but your personal home, personal bank accounts, and other assets are protected. Without an LLC, everything you own is fair game in a lawsuit. That's a risk you simply cannot afford to take.

Setting up an LLC is relatively simple and inexpensive. You can do it through your state's Secretary of State office, and it typically costs a few hundred dollars. Some investors create a separate LLC for each property they own. Others hold multiple properties in a single LLC. The right structure depends on your situation, and I recommend consulting with a real estate attorney who can advise you based on the laws in your state.

Beyond LLCs, there are other entities to consider as your wealth grows—S corporations, trusts, and family limited partnerships. Each serves a different purpose and offers different advantages. As your portfolio grows, your legal structure should grow with it.

The key takeaway is this: never hold investment assets in your personal name. Always use a legal entity to protect yourself. It's one of the simplest yet most important steps you can take to safeguard your wealth.

Insurance: Your Financial Shield

Insurance is another critical layer of protection. And I'm not just talking about the basic homeowner's policy. As an investor and business owner, you need comprehensive coverage that addresses the unique risks you face.

For rental properties, you need landlord insurance—not a standard homeowner's policy. Landlord insurance covers property damage, liability claims, and lost rental income. It's specifically designed for properties that are rented to tenants, and it's essential.

You should also consider an umbrella insurance policy. An umbrella policy provides an extra layer of liability coverage beyond what your individual property and auto policies offer. If a judgment against you exceeds the limits of your standard policy, the umbrella kicks in. For the relatively low cost of an umbrella policy, the additional protection is well worth it.

If you own a business, you'll need general liability insurance, and depending on your industry, you may need professional liability insurance, workers' compensation, or commercial property insurance.

As your wealth grows, you should also think about life insurance—particularly a term life policy that provides for your family if something happens to you. And if you have dependents, disability insurance is equally important, because an injury or illness that prevents you from working can be just as financially devastating as death.

The point isn't to be fearful—it's to be wise. Proverbs 27:12 reminds us that a prudent person sees danger and takes precautions. Insurance is one of those precautions. It doesn't prevent bad things from happening, but it ensures that when they do, your wealth survives intact.

Estate Planning: Securing the Transfer

Here's a sobering truth: if you don't have an estate plan, the government has one for you—and you're not going to like it. Without a will or a trust, your assets will be distributed according to state law when you pass away. That process—called probate—is public, time-consuming, expensive, and often doesn't reflect your wishes.

Estate planning is how you ensure that the wealth you've built gets transferred to the people you choose, in the way you choose, with as little tax and legal friction as possible.

At a minimum, every adult should have a will. A will specifies who gets your assets, who takes care of your minor children, and who manages your estate after you're gone. Without one, the courts make those decisions for you.

A living trust offers additional advantages. Assets held in a trust bypass probate entirely, which means faster distribution, lower costs, and more privacy. A trust also allows you to set conditions on how and when your beneficiaries receive their inheritance—for example, you can stipulate that your children don't receive their full inheritance until they reach a certain age or complete their education.

You should also have a power of attorney—someone authorized to make financial decisions on your behalf if you become incapacitated—and a healthcare directive that outlines your medical wishes.

I know this isn't the most exciting topic, but please don't skip this step. I've seen families torn apart by the absence of an estate plan. I've seen fortunes evaporate in probate court. I've seen children left with nothing because their parents never took the time to put their wishes in writing.

You're building wealth for your family. Make sure it actually gets to them.

Tax Strategy: Keeping More of What You Earn

Let me tell you something that might surprise you: the wealthy don't necessarily earn more money than everyone else. They keep more of what they earn. And they do that through strategic tax planning.

The tax code is thousands of pages long, and buried within those pages are dozens of legal strategies that can significantly reduce your tax burden. Real estate investors, in particular, have access to some of the most powerful tax benefits available.

Depreciation allows you to deduct a portion of a property's value each year as a paper loss—even if the property is actually going up in value. This can offset your rental income and sometimes even your other income, reducing your overall tax bill.

The 1031 exchange allows you to sell an investment property and defer the capital gains taxes by reinvesting the proceeds into another property. This lets your money continue to grow without giving a chunk of it to the government.

Retirement accounts like self-directed IRAs and Solo 401(k)s allow you to invest in real estate using tax-advantaged dollars. The growth inside these accounts is either tax-deferred or tax-free, depending on the type of account.

Business deductions allow you to write off legitimate expenses like home office costs, vehicle use, education, professional services, and travel. As a business owner and investor, your tax situation is fundamentally different from someone who only earns a W-2 salary.

The key is to work with a qualified CPA or tax strategist—not just someone who files returns, but someone who proactively plans your tax strategy throughout the year. A good tax advisor can save you thousands of dollars annually, and that money can be redirected into your investments and your legacy.

Here's the bottom line: building wealth is only half the equation. Protecting it is the other half. Legal entities, insurance, estate planning, and tax strategy are the four pillars of financial protection. Without them, your wealth is built on sand. With them, it's built on rock.

And I think Jesus had something to say about building on rock versus sand. Matthew 7:24–25 says, "The rain came down, the streams rose, and the winds blew and beat against that house; yet it did not fall, because it had its foundation on the rock."

Build your financial house on the rock. Protect what God has blessed you to build. Because this isn't just about you—it's about every generation that comes after you.

Don't miss this. Take action now. Set up your LLC. Review your insurance. Call an estate planning attorney. Meet with a tax strategist. These are the moves that separate people who build temporary wealth from people who build lasting legacies.

Your future heirs are counting on you. Don't let them down.

Reflection and Action Steps

Protection isn't exciting, but it's essential. Here's your checklist for the next thirty days.

First, if you own any investment property or business, look into forming an LLC if you haven't already. Research the requirements in your state and budget for the filing fee. If you're unsure, schedule a consultation with a real estate or business attorney. Many offer free initial consultations.

Second, review your insurance coverage. Are you adequately covered for your properties, your business, and your personal life? Do you have an umbrella policy? If not, get quotes this week. The cost is often surprisingly affordable for the amount of protection it provides.

Third, if you don't have a will or a trust, schedule an appointment with an estate planning attorney. I know this feels morbid, but it's one of the most loving things you can do for your family. Make sure your wishes are documented and your assets are positioned to transfer smoothly.

Fourth, schedule a meeting with a CPA or tax strategist—not just a tax preparer, but someone who proactively plans your tax strategy. Ask them about depreciation, 1031 exchanges, retirement accounts, and any other strategies that could reduce your tax burden.

Doing these four things will put you ahead of ninety percent of people who build wealth without protecting it. Don't be the person who builds a castle on sand. Build on rock. Protect what God has blessed you to create.

The Protection Mindset

I want to leave you with a mindset shift about protection. Most people think of protection as reactive—something you worry about after you've built something worth protecting. But the most successful wealth-builders think about protection proactively. They build the protective structures alongside the wealth, not after it.

Think about it like building a house. You don't pour the foundation, frame the walls, install the plumbing, and finish the interior—and then think about the roof. The roof is part of the plan from day one. It's not an afterthought. It's integral to the structure.

Your LLC, your insurance, your estate plan, and your tax strategy are the roof of your financial house. Without them, everything inside is exposed to the elements. With them, what you've built is secure.

I've seen people build incredible wealth and lose it because they treated protection as optional. A single lawsuit wiped out their portfolio because they didn't have an LLC. A sudden death devastated their family because there was no estate plan. A massive tax bill consumed their profits because they never hired a strategist.

Don't let that be your story. Build the protective structures now—even before your wealth is significant. Because the habits and systems you establish early will scale with you as your wealth grows. Starting an LLC when you own one property is much simpler than restructuring when you own ten.

Protection isn't paranoia. It's wisdom. And wisdom is the companion of every successful heir.

PART THREE: LEGACY — PASSING THE TORCH

CHAPTER 11

Teach Your Children Well

"Train up a child in the way he should go; even when he is old he will not depart from it." — Proverbs 22:6

Everything we've talked about so far—the mindset, the strategies, the protection—means nothing if the next generation doesn't know what to do with it. You can build the biggest portfolio in the world, but if your children don't understand money, they'll burn through it faster than you built it.

Statistics tell us that seventy percent of wealthy families lose their wealth by the second generation. By the third generation, that number jumps to ninety percent. Ninety percent. That means almost everything you build could be gone within your grandchildren's lifetime—not because the money wasn't there, but because the knowledge wasn't transferred.

That is unacceptable. And it's preventable.

The number one thing you can do to ensure your wealth lasts beyond your lifetime is to teach your children about money. Not someday. Not when they're older. Now. Start the conversations now. Model the behaviors now. Create the habits now.

I know what some of you are thinking: "My kids are too young to understand money." But I'd push back on that. Children understand more than we give them credit for. A five-year-old can learn to save money in a jar. A ten-year-old can understand the difference between a need and a want. A teenager can learn to manage a bank account, invest small amounts, and make smart spending decisions.

The question isn't whether they're ready. The question is whether you're willing to teach them.

Making Money Conversations Normal

In many families, money is a taboo subject. We'll talk about politics, religion, health—but money? That's off-limits. And that silence is one of the biggest reasons financial illiteracy gets passed down from one generation to the next.

If your children never hear you talk about budgeting, investing, saving, and giving, how will they learn? If they never see you sit down and review your finances, how will they develop the habit? If they never participate in financial decisions—even small ones—how will they build the skills they need to manage wealth?

You have to make money conversations a normal part of your family life. That doesn't mean sharing every detail of your financial situation with your six-year-old. But it does mean creating age-appropriate opportunities for your children to learn about how money works.

When you're at the grocery store, talk to your kids about prices and value. When you pay bills, let them see the process. When you're making a big purchase, involve them in the decision. Explain why you're choosing one option over another. Explain the concept of saving up for something instead of buying it on credit.

As your children get older, the conversations should deepen. Teach your teenagers about credit scores, interest rates, and the power of compound growth. Help them open a bank account and a small investment account. Let them make financial mistakes with small amounts while the stakes are low so they can learn before the stakes are high.

The families that build lasting wealth are the ones that talk about money openly, honestly, and often. Don't let silence rob your children of the financial education they deserve.

Creating Financially Literate Heirs

Beyond conversations, there are practical steps you can take to ensure your children develop true financial literacy.

Give them an allowance—but not for free. Tie it to chores, responsibilities, or entrepreneurial activities. Teach them that money is earned through effort and value creation. Then help them divide that allowance into three categories: saving, giving, and spending. This simple framework teaches them stewardship from a young age.

Encourage entrepreneurship. Some of the most valuable financial lessons come from starting a small business. Whether it's a lemonade stand, a lawn care service, or selling handmade crafts online, entrepreneurship teaches children about profit, expenses, customer service, and problem-solving—skills that will serve them for the rest of their lives.

Introduce them to investing early—especially real estate. Take your children to see your rental properties. Walk them through how rent comes in, how expenses go out, and what cash flow means in real numbers. Let them sit in on a property analysis. When they're old enough, involve them in a renovation project or let them help screen tenant applications. There are also platforms that allow minors to own fractional shares of stocks and REITs with parental oversight. Buying your child a few shares of a company they know and love—like their favorite clothing brand or tech company—makes investing tangible and exciting. Let them track the price, learn about what the company does, and experience the reality of markets going up and down.

Model generosity. Let your children see you tithe. Let them see you give to those in need. Let them participate in charitable giving. When children learn that money is a tool for blessing others, they develop a healthy, purpose-driven relationship with wealth.

And perhaps most importantly, model what you're preaching. Your children are watching everything you do. If you tell them to save but you spend impulsively, they'll do what they see, not what they hear. If you tell them to invest but you never do it yourself, the lesson won't stick. Be the example. Live the principles. Show them what faithful stewardship looks like in real time.

The greatest inheritance you can leave your children isn't money. It's the wisdom to manage it. Give them both, and you've given them everything.

The Family Wealth Meeting

One of the most powerful tools I recommend to families who are serious about building generational wealth is the family wealth meeting. This is a regular, structured time where your family comes together to talk about finances, goals, values, and legacy.

Think of it like a board meeting for your family's financial future. You review where you stand, where you're headed, and what each person's role is in the journey. Younger children can participate at their level—learning about goals and saving—while older children and teens can be involved in discussions about investments, budgets, and long-term plans.

The family wealth meeting serves multiple purposes. It keeps everyone on the same page. It creates accountability. It builds a culture of financial awareness and responsibility. And it sends a powerful message to your children: this family takes money seriously, and you are part of the team.

Hold these meetings monthly or quarterly. Make them casual but intentional. Start with a prayer—invite God into the process. Review your family budget. Discuss any upcoming expenses. Talk about progress toward savings and investment goals. Celebrate wins, no matter how small. And always end with a vision for the future—remind your family of why you're doing this and what you're building together.

Over time, these meetings become a family tradition. They become the backbone of your family's financial culture. And when your children grow up and start their own families, they'll bring this habit with them—because it's all they've ever known.

That's how legacies are built. Not just with money, but with habits. Not just with assets, but with values. Not just with wealth, but with wisdom.

So here's your challenge: schedule your first family wealth meeting this month. It doesn't have to be fancy. It just has to happen. Start the conversation. Set the tone. And watch how it transforms your family's relationship with money.

Your children are your greatest investment. Invest in them wisely.

Reflection and Action Steps

Teaching your children about money starts today—regardless of their age. Here's how to start.

If your children are under ten, introduce the concept of saving, giving, and spending with three labeled jars or envelopes. Give them a small amount of money each week tied to age-appropriate responsibilities, and help them divide it into the three categories. Make it fun and celebrate when they reach a savings goal.

If your children are between ten and fifteen, open a bank account in their name with parental oversight. Teach them to track their balance, understand interest, and set savings goals. Start introducing the concept of investing by buying them a few shares of a company they know and love.

If your children are teenagers, involve them in real family financial discussions. Show them a utility bill and explain how it fits into the budget. Let them sit in on a meeting with your financial advisor. Help them get their first job or start a small business. Teach them about credit before they turn eighteen so they can start building a strong score from day one.

And regardless of age, schedule your first family wealth meeting this month. It can be fifteen minutes over pizza. The format doesn't matter. What matters is that the conversation starts.

Your children are watching. Make sure what they see is worth imitating.

Beyond Financial Literacy: Teaching Values

Financial literacy gives your children the skills to manage money. But values give them the wisdom to use it well. Without values, even the most financially literate person can make destructive choices with their wealth.

So what values should you intentionally instill in the next generation?

First, stewardship—the understanding that everything belongs to God and we are managers, not owners. When your children understand this, they'll approach money with humility and responsibility rather than entitlement and recklessness.

Second, generosity—the habit of giving freely and joyfully. Children who learn to give early develop a healthy detachment from money. They understand that money is a tool for blessing, not a source of identity or security.

Third, delayed gratification—the ability to wait for a greater reward rather than grabbing what's available now. In a world of instant everything—instant delivery, instant streaming, instant credit—delayed gratification is a superpower. Teach your children to save for what they want rather than buying it on impulse.

Fourth, hard work—the conviction that effort produces reward and that nothing of value comes without it. Let your children earn their money through chores, jobs, or small businesses. Don't just hand them everything. The lessons learned through effort are lessons that stick.

Fifth, faith—the foundation that holds everything else together. When your children understand that God is their provider, they can face financial challenges without panic. They can make bold moves without paralyzing fear. They can give generously without scarcity thinking.

Teach these values not just through words but through your life. Let your children see you save, give, work hard, wait patiently, and trust God with your finances. That example will speak louder than any lecture you could ever deliver.

Age-Appropriate Money Conversations

One question I get asked all the time is, "What should I teach my kids about money at different ages?" So let me give you a practical breakdown.

Ages three to five: This is the introduction phase. Children at this age can understand basic concepts like trading money for things. Use a clear jar for savings so they can see the money grow. Play store with them—let them "buy" items with pretend money. Read children's books about money and saving. The goal isn't financial literacy—it's financial familiarity.

Ages six to ten: This is the foundation phase. Introduce an allowance tied to responsibilities. Use the three-jar system—save, give, spend—and let them make real choices about how to allocate their money. Take them shopping and let them compare prices. When they want something, help them save for it rather than buying it immediately. Start explaining the basics of how banks work, what interest means, and why saving matters.

Ages eleven to fourteen: This is the application phase. Open a bank account in their name. Teach them to track deposits and withdrawals. Introduce the concept of investing—buy them a share of stock in a company they love and let them watch it grow (or shrink). Start taking them to see rental properties. Let them sit in on a deal analysis so they begin to understand how real estate generates income. Discuss needs versus wants in real-world scenarios. Start talking about how credit works and why it matters. Let them earn money through small entrepreneurial activities—mowing lawns, babysitting, selling handmade items.

Ages fifteen to eighteen: This is the preparation phase. Add them as an authorized user on a credit card to start building their credit history. Teach them to file a basic tax return. Involve them in real financial decisions—show them the mortgage statement, the insurance bill, the investment account. Walk them through your real estate portfolio and explain how each property contributes to the family's wealth. Discuss career choices through the lens of income potential and fulfillment. Help them create their first budget and first financial goal.

At every age, the most important thing you can do is be open, honest, and consistent. Make money a normal topic of conversation, not a source of stress or secrecy. When you normalize financial discussions, you raise children who are comfortable and confident with money—and that comfort is one of the greatest gifts you can give them.

CHAPTER 12

Building Wealth as a Family

"Two are better than one, because they have a good return for their labor." — Ecclesiastes 4:9

Wealth building shouldn't be a solo sport. The families that build the greatest fortunes don't do it individually—they do it collectively. They pool resources, share knowledge, divide responsibilities, and move together toward a common vision.

Think about some of the wealthiest families in history. The Rockefellers. The Rothschilds. The Waltons. What do they all have in common? They built as a family. They created systems, structures, and cultures that allowed each generation to contribute to and benefit from the family's collective wealth.

Now, you don't need to be a Rockefeller to apply this principle. Whether your family has a lot or a little, the concept of building wealth as a unit is incredibly powerful. When a family aligns around a shared financial vision, the results are exponentially greater than what any single family member could achieve alone.

In this chapter, I want to explore what it looks like to build wealth as a family—practically, strategically, and spiritually.

Getting on the Same Page with Your Spouse

If you're married, your spouse is your most important financial partner. And if you're not on the same page financially, you're going to struggle—no matter how good your strategy is.

Money is one of the leading causes of conflict in marriages. And in most cases, the conflict isn't really about the money—it's about values, priorities, and communication. One person is a saver and the other is a spender. One person wants to invest aggressively and the other wants to play it safe. One person wants to talk about money and the other avoids the subject entirely.

If any of that sounds familiar, you're not alone. My wife and I had to work through every one of those dynamics. There were arguments, misunderstandings, and seasons where we were pulling in different directions. But over time, we learned to communicate, to compromise, and to align around a shared vision for our family's financial future.

Here's what worked for us. First, we got honest about our individual relationships with money. We talked about how we were raised, what money meant to us, and what our fears and hopes were. That level of vulnerability created understanding and empathy. Second, we agreed on shared goals. We sat down and defined what financial freedom looked like for our family—and we wrote it down. Third, we divided responsibilities based on our strengths. I handle the investing and deal analysis; she manages our household budget and keeps us on track with our savings goals. We play to our strengths and respect each other's contributions.

If you and your spouse aren't aligned financially, that's the first thing you need to address. Have the conversation. Be honest. Be patient. And remember—you're on the same team. The enemy is not each other. The enemy is financial ignorance and misalignment.

Family Business and Collective Economics

One of the most powerful ways to build wealth as a family is to create and grow a family business. A business owned and operated by family members keeps money circulating within the family, creates employment for family members, and can be passed down from generation to generation.

A family business doesn't have to be a massive corporation. It could be a rental property portfolio managed by the family. It could be a catering company, a landscaping service, a cleaning business, or a consulting firm. The key is that the business creates value, generates income, and involves multiple family members in its growth and success.

I've also seen families practice collective economics—pooling money together to make investments they couldn't make individually. For example, four siblings each contribute ten thousand dollars to create a forty-thousand-dollar investment fund. They use that money to purchase a rental property, share the management responsibilities, and split the profits. What none of them could do alone, they accomplish together.

This isn't a new concept. Cultures around the world have practiced collective economics for centuries. Rotating savings groups, community lending circles, and family investment clubs have helped countless families build wealth from modest means. There's immense power in pooling resources when you share trust, transparency, and a common goal.

If your family is open to it, consider starting a family investment club. Meet monthly, pool a set amount of money, research opportunities together, and make investment decisions as a group. It's an incredible way to build wealth, strengthen family bonds, and create a legacy of financial collaboration.

Family Trusts and Wealth Structures

As your family's wealth grows, you'll want to create formal structures to manage, protect, and distribute it. This is where family trusts and other wealth management tools come into play.

A family trust is a legal entity that holds assets on behalf of your family members. It can include real estate, investments, business interests, cash, and other assets. The trust is managed by a trustee—which can be you, a family member, or a professional—according to the rules you set when you create it.

The benefits of a family trust are significant. It protects assets from creditors and lawsuits. It allows for controlled distribution—you can specify that your children receive their inheritance at certain ages or milestones, rather than all at once. It avoids probate, which saves time and money. And it provides a framework for multi-generational wealth management.

Another tool to consider is a family limited partnership, or FLP. This is a legal structure where parents serve as general partners and children serve as limited partners. The parents maintain control over the assets while gradually transferring ownership—and the associated wealth—to the children. This can be an effective way to transfer wealth while minimizing gift and estate taxes.

These are sophisticated strategies, and I strongly recommend working with an estate planning attorney and a financial advisor who specialize in family wealth. The upfront cost of setting up these structures is a fraction of what they'll save your family over the long term.

Here's the bottom line: if you're serious about building generational wealth, you need generational structures. A family that builds wealth without a plan for transferring it is like a farmer who plants a crop but never harvests. The work is wasted.

Build the wealth. Build the structure. And build the family culture that holds it all together.

Remember, God rewards those who trust Him and take bold steps forward. Building wealth as a family is one of the boldest and most beautiful things you can do. It requires vulnerability, communication, and a shared commitment to something bigger than any one person.

But the reward is worth it. A family united around a vision of generational prosperity is an unstoppable force. Be that family. Start today.

Reflection and Action Steps

Building wealth as a family requires intentional communication and structure. Here's how to start.

First, if you're married or in a partnership, schedule a money date this week. Not a budget review—a conversation about your dreams, your fears, and your vision for your family's financial future. Listen more than you speak. Seek to understand before seeking to be understood.

Second, identify one way your family can pool resources for a shared financial goal. Maybe it's saving together for a family investment property. Maybe it's starting a family savings challenge. Maybe it's contributing to a family education fund. The specific goal matters less than the act of building together.

Third, research one wealth management structure—a family trust, an LLC, or a family limited partnership—and learn the basics. You don't need to set one up tomorrow, but understanding your options now will prepare you for when the time is right.

Fourth, consider starting a family investment club with extended family members who share your vision. Set clear rules, contribute consistently, and make decisions together. It's one of the most powerful ways to accelerate wealth-building while strengthening family bonds.

Remember, you don't have to build alone. God designed the family as a wealth-building unit. Lean into that design. Build together. Win together. Leave a legacy together.

Navigating Family Dynamics and Money

Let's get real about something: families and money can be a volatile combination. Even the closest families can experience tension, conflict, and hurt feelings when money enters the picture.

Maybe you've experienced this yourself. A family member borrowed money and never paid it back. A disagreement about an inheritance tore siblings apart. A business partnership with a relative went south and damaged the relationship.

These situations are painful, but they're not inevitable. The key to navigating family dynamics and money is structure, communication, and boundaries.

Structure means putting agreements in writing—even with family. Especially with family. If you're lending money to a relative, create a written agreement with terms, a repayment schedule, and consequences for default. If you're partnering with a family member in a business or investment, draft a formal partnership agreement. These documents aren't signs of distrust—they're signs of wisdom. They protect the relationship by ensuring everyone is on the same page.

Communication means having regular, honest conversations about money—expectations, concerns, goals, and challenges. The family wealth meeting I discussed in the previous chapter is one tool for this. But it also means being willing to have the uncomfortable one-on-one conversations when issues arise, rather than letting resentment build.

Boundaries mean knowing when to say no. You can love your family and still decline to fund every request. You can be generous and still have limits. You can support your relatives and still protect your own financial future. Setting boundaries isn't selfish—it's sustainable. Because if you give until you're depleted, you won't be able to help anyone—including yourself.

Building wealth as a family is beautiful, but it requires maturity, communication, and grace. Approach it with wisdom, and it will strengthen your family bonds rather than strain them.

CHAPTER 13

The Power of Community and Kingdom Networks

"As iron sharpens iron, so one person sharpens another." — Proverbs 27:17

I've said it before and I'll say it again: you cannot build generational wealth alone. It takes a village—or in our case, it takes a kingdom network.

Every major success in my life has been connected to a relationship. The mentor who showed me my first real estate deal. The partner who helped me fund a project I couldn't afford alone. The friend who introduced me to a lender who said yes when everyone else said no. The community of believers who prayed for me when deals fell through and celebrated with me when they closed.

None of this happened in isolation. And your wealth-building journey won't happen in isolation either.

The truth is, the people around you have a profound impact on your trajectory. If you're surrounded by people who are building, investing, and growing, you'll naturally rise to that level. If you're surrounded by people who are stuck, complaining, and making excuses, you'll find it incredibly difficult to break free—no matter how motivated you are.

That's not judgment. That's reality. And it's why being intentional about your community is one of the most important decisions you'll make on this journey.

Finding Your Tribe

So where do you find a community of like-minded believers who are serious about building wealth? Here are a few places to start.

Local real estate investment groups are goldmines for networking. Most cities have at least one group that meets regularly—sometimes weekly—to discuss deals, strategies, and opportunities. These groups are full of people at every level, from beginners to seasoned investors. Show up consistently, ask questions, and build relationships. You'll be amazed at the opportunities that come your way.

Church-based financial groups and ministries are another great option. Many churches offer financial literacy classes, wealth-building workshops, or small groups focused on biblical stewardship. If your church doesn't have one, consider starting one. You'd be surprised how many people in your congregation are hungry for financial wisdom but don't know where to turn.

Online communities have exploded in recent years. There are Facebook groups, forums, and membership communities dedicated to every niche of investing and business-building. These digital spaces allow you to connect with people across the country—and around the world—who share your goals and values.

Masterminds and mentorship groups offer a more focused, high-touch form of community. A mastermind is a small group of individuals who meet regularly to share challenges, brainstorm solutions, and hold each other accountable. Being part of a mastermind can accelerate your growth exponentially because you're consistently exposed to diverse perspectives and higher-level thinking.

For real estate investors specifically, your network is everything. The best deals rarely show up on listing sites—they come through relationships. The investor who hears about an off-market property at a networking meeting. The mentor who introduces you to a private money lender. The fellow believer who partners with you on a deal you couldn't do alone. In real estate, your network literally determines the quality of deals you have access to.

Whatever form your community takes, the key is consistency. Don't just show up once and disappear. Build real relationships. Be genuinely interested in other people's journeys. Offer value before you ask for it. The strongest networks are built on trust and mutual support, not on what you can extract from someone.

The Kingdom Economy

As believers, we have access to something beyond a natural economy—we have access to the kingdom economy. The kingdom economy operates on different principles than the world's system. It's built on generosity, reciprocity, faithfulness, and the supernatural provision of God.

In the world's economy, you hoard to get ahead. In the kingdom economy, you give to get ahead. Luke 6:38 says, "Give, and it will be given to you. A good measure, pressed down, shaken together and running over, will be poured into your lap." That's not just a spiritual platitude—it's an economic principle.

I've experienced this firsthand. Some of my biggest financial breakthroughs have come right after seasons of significant generosity. Not because I was trying to earn something from God, but because generosity positions your heart to receive. When you're open-handed with what you have, God knows He can trust you with more.

The kingdom economy also operates through divine connections. God has a way of putting the right people in your path at exactly the right time. That unexpected introduction, that "random" conversation at church, that connection at a networking event—those aren't coincidences. Those are kingdom setups.

But you have to be positioned to receive them. You have to be in the room. You have to be building relationships. You have to be open to opportunities that don't look like what you expected.

Being a Connector and a Blessing

Here's a principle that will serve you well in every area of life: be a connector, not just a collector. Don't just network to benefit yourself—network to benefit others. When you meet someone who needs help, connect them with someone who can provide it. When you learn something valuable, share it freely. When you have the opportunity to lift someone else up, do it without hesitation.

The people who build the strongest networks are the ones who are known for adding value to every room they enter. They're not just asking, "What can you do for me?" They're asking, "How can I serve you?"

I've made it a practice to make at least one introduction every week—connecting two people in my network who could benefit from knowing each other. It costs me nothing but a few minutes of thought and a text message. But the goodwill it generates is immeasurable. People remember the person who connected them with an opportunity, a resource, or a relationship that changed their life.

And that's what the kingdom is all about. We're not in competition with each other—we're in collaboration. There's more than enough for everyone. When one of us wins, all of us win. When one of us grows, it creates opportunity for others to grow too.

So build your community with intention. Show up generously. Serve faithfully. And trust that God will multiply the seeds you plant in the lives of others.

Here's the bottom line: your network is your net worth. Not just financially, but relationally and spiritually. Surround yourself with people who challenge you, encourage you, and hold you accountable. And be that person for someone else.

This is how the kingdom grows—one relationship, one connection, one act of service at a time.

You were never meant to do this alone. Find your tribe. Build your network. And watch what God does when His people move together in faith and purpose.

Reflection and Action Steps

Your network won't build itself. Here's your plan for the next thirty days.

First, identify and attend one networking event—a real estate investment group, a business meetup, a church financial ministry, or an online community meeting. Go with the intention of learning and connecting, not selling or pitching. Introduce yourself to at least three new people and follow up with each of them within forty-eight hours.

Second, identify one person who is further along the wealth-building journey than you and ask them to mentor you. Be specific in your ask. Don't just say, "Will you be my mentor?" Instead, say, "I admire what you've built. Could I buy you coffee once a month and ask you questions about your journey?" Most people are honored to be asked and happy to share.

Third, make one introduction this week. Think of two people in your network who could benefit from knowing each other and connect them. The habit of connecting others builds your reputation as a giver, not just a taker, and it creates goodwill that comes back to you in unexpected ways.

Fourth, evaluate your current circle. Are the five people you spend the most time with pulling you up or holding you back? This isn't about cutting people off—it's about adding people who challenge and inspire you. You don't have to leave anyone behind. You just need to expand your circle forward.

Your community is one of your greatest assets. Invest in it intentionally, and it will pay dividends for the rest of your life.

Digital Community and Modern Networking

We live in an age where your next business partner, mentor, or investor could be on the other side of the country—or the other side of the world. Digital community has expanded the possibilities for networking in ways that previous generations couldn't have imagined.

Social media, when used intentionally, is a powerful networking tool. Share your journey. Document your wins and your lessons. Engage authentically with others who are on similar paths. I've seen deals, partnerships, and mentorship relationships form entirely through social media connections.

Online courses and masterminds create focused communities around shared learning goals. When you invest in a course or program, you're not just buying information—you're buying access to a community of people who are all investing in their growth at the same time. Some of the most valuable connections in my life have come from paid communities where everyone was serious about leveling up.

Virtual meetups and webinars allow you to learn from and connect with experts regardless of geography. Many real estate investment groups, business organizations, and faith-based financial ministries now offer virtual events that you can attend from your living room.

But here's my caution: digital community should supplement, not replace, face-to-face relationships. There's something irreplaceable about sitting across the table from someone, shaking their hand, and looking them in the eye. The strongest business relationships are built on personal connection—and that requires in-person time.

Use digital tools to expand your reach, but invest in local relationships to deepen your roots. The combination of broad reach and deep roots creates a network that can support you through anything the journey throws your way.

CHAPTER 14

Giving Back: Tithing, Philanthropy, and Purpose

"Whoever is kind to the poor lends to the Lord, and he will reward them for what they have done." — Proverbs 19:17

Let me ask you a question that might seem counterintuitive in a book about building wealth: are you ready to give it away?

I know that sounds crazy. We've spent the last thirteen chapters talking about how to earn it, grow it, invest it, and protect it. And now I'm asking you to give it away? Absolutely. Because here's a truth that the world will never teach you: generosity is not the enemy of wealth. Generosity is the accelerator of wealth.

Every wealthy person of faith I've ever met has one thing in common: they give. They give generously, they give consistently, and they give joyfully. Not because they're trying to buy God's blessing, but because they understand a fundamental spiritual law—when you sow, you reap. When you open your hand, God opens His hand. When you trust Him with your resources, He trusts you with more.

This isn't a get-rich-quick scheme. It's a kingdom principle that has been operating since the beginning of time. And if you want to build wealth that truly matters—wealth that has eternal impact—you have to build generosity into the foundation.

The Power of the Tithe

Tithing—giving ten percent of your income to your local church—is one of the most debated topics in Christendom. Some people believe it's an Old Testament principle that doesn't apply today. Others believe it's the foundation of faithful financial stewardship.

I'm not going to argue theology with you. What I am going to tell you is this: tithing has been one of the most transformative practices in my financial life. And I've heard the same thing from countless other believers.

When I started tithing consistently, something shifted. It wasn't magical or immediate. But over time, I noticed that my finances became more ordered, more fruitful, and more blessed. Opportunities showed up that I couldn't have manufactured. Bills got paid that I wasn't sure how I'd cover. Deals came together that defied logic.

Was it because God was rewarding my tithing? I believe so. Malachi 3:10 is the only place in the Bible where God says, "Test me in this." He invites us to try it and see what happens. And in my experience, when you honor God with the first portion of your income, He takes care of the rest in ways you can't explain.

But tithing isn't just about what God does for you. It's about what it does in you. Tithing trains you to hold your money loosely. It reminds you that everything you have belongs to God. It builds your faith muscle by requiring you to trust God with your finances in a tangible way. And it positions your heart to receive more, because God knows you'll steward it well.

If you're not tithing right now, I challenge you to start. Start where you are—even if it's uncomfortable. Watch what happens over the next six months, the next year, the next five years. I believe you'll look back and see God's hand all over your finances.

Beyond the Tithe: Strategic Generosity

The tithe is the floor, not the ceiling. Once you've established a tithing habit, God will begin to open your eyes to opportunities for generosity that go beyond ten percent.

Strategic generosity means being intentional about how, where, and to whom you give. It means aligning your giving with your values and your vision. Some people are passionate about education and choose to fund scholarships. Others are passionate about housing and invest in affordable housing initiatives. Some are drawn to missions and support work in communities around the world. Others are passionate about their local community and fund programs that serve their neighbors.

When you give strategically, your money has maximum impact. You're not just throwing dollars at problems—you're investing in solutions that align with your God-given purpose.

I've also learned that generosity doesn't always mean writing a check. Sometimes the most generous thing you can do is give your time. Mentor a young person who's where you used to be. Volunteer your skills to a nonprofit. Teach a financial literacy class at your church. Share your knowledge freely with people who need it.

Generosity creates a ripple effect. When you bless someone, they're in a better position to bless someone else. And that chain of blessing can extend far beyond what you can see. You may never know the full impact of a single act of generosity—but God does.

Purpose-Driven Wealth

Here's the big picture: wealth without purpose is empty. You can have a million dollars in the bank, but if it's not connected to something bigger than yourself, it's just a number on a screen.

I've met people who chased money for its own sake, and when they got it, they felt emptier than before. Because money can buy comfort, but it can't buy meaning. Money can buy security, but it can't buy purpose. Money can buy influence, but it can't buy fulfillment.

True wealth—the kind this book is about—is wealth with purpose. It's wealth that serves God's kingdom. It's wealth that blesses your family, strengthens your community, and changes lives. It's wealth that has an eternal dimension to it.

When you connect your wealth to God's purpose for your life, everything comes into alignment. Your work has meaning. Your investments have impact. Your generosity has power. And your legacy has depth.

So I want you to think about this: why are you building wealth? Not just the surface-level answer—dig deeper. What is God calling you to fund? What problem is He asking you to solve? What community is He asking you to serve? What cause is He placing on your heart?

Your answer to those questions is the purpose behind your wealth. And when you build with purpose, you build with power.

First Timothy 6:17–19 puts it beautifully. It tells the wealthy to not be arrogant or put their hope in wealth, which is so uncertain. Instead, they should put their hope in God, who richly provides us with everything for our enjoyment. They should do good, be rich in good deeds, and be generous and willing to share. In this way, they lay up treasure for themselves as a firm foundation for the coming age.

That's the vision. Build wealth, be generous, and lay up eternal treasure. Not because you have to, but because you get to. Because God has entrusted you with resources and the opportunity to make a difference.

Here's my challenge to you: as you build your wealth, build your generosity alongside it. Don't wait until you're "rich enough" to start giving. Start now. Give from where you are. Trust God with it. And watch Him multiply both your resources and your impact.

This is your moment to build something that matters—something that outlasts you and blesses generations you'll never meet. That's purpose-driven wealth. That's The HEIRS™ way.

Reflection and Action Steps

Generosity is a muscle—the more you exercise it, the stronger it gets. Here's your generosity workout for this month.

First, if you're not currently tithing, make a commitment to start. Begin with whatever percentage feels like a stretch—even if it's not the full ten percent yet. Set up an automatic recurring donation to your church so it happens consistently without you having to think about it each time.

Second, identify one cause or organization that aligns with your values and make a one-time gift. It doesn't have to be a large amount. What matters is the intentionality behind it. Research where your money goes and how it's used. Strategic giving multiplies your impact.

Third, give your time. Volunteer for one event, one class, or one mentoring session this month. Share your knowledge, your experience, or simply your presence with someone who needs it. Time is often more valuable than money, and the relational return on volunteering is immeasurable.

Fourth, write down your why. Why are you building wealth? What purpose does it serve beyond your own comfort? When your wealth is connected to a purpose bigger than yourself, it takes on a power and a significance that transforms not just your bank account but your entire life.

God has blessed you to be a blessing. Go be one.

Creating a Family Giving Strategy

Just as you have an investment strategy and a wealth-protection strategy, I believe every family should have a giving strategy. Intentional generosity is far more impactful than reactive generosity.

A family giving strategy starts with identifying your family's core values and passions. What breaks your heart? What lights your fire? Where do you see the greatest need? Maybe it's education in underserved communities. Maybe it's affordable housing. Maybe it's supporting missionaries or fighting food insecurity. Your giving should reflect what your family cares about most.

Next, decide on a giving budget. This includes your tithe to your local church, but it can also include a separate allocation for charitable giving. As your income grows, consider increasing this allocation. Some families set a goal of giving away a certain percentage beyond the tithe—fifteen percent, twenty percent, or even more—as their wealth increases.

Then, research organizations and causes that align with your values. Look for transparency, accountability, and measurable impact. Not all nonprofits are created equal, and your giving dollars should go where they'll make the biggest difference.

Finally, involve your children in the giving process. Let them help choose causes to support. Take them to volunteer at organizations you fund. Show them the impact of generosity firsthand. When children experience the joy of giving, it becomes part of who they are—not just something their parents do.

A family giving strategy transforms generosity from an occasional act into a lifestyle. It makes giving intentional, impactful, and sustainable. And it teaches the next generation that wealth is not just for accumulation—it's for transformation.

CHAPTER 15

Your Legacy Starts Now

"A good person leaves an inheritance for their children's children." — Proverbs 13:22

We've come a long way together. Fifteen chapters. Three parts. Hundreds of pages of mindset shifts, practical strategies, and faith-driven wisdom. But this last chapter isn't the end. It's the beginning.

Everything you've read in this book is useless if it stays on these pages. The strategies don't work unless you work them. The principles don't produce results unless you apply them. The vision doesn't become reality unless you act on it.

So this final chapter is both a culmination and a commissioning. It's where we bring everything together into a cohesive plan for your family's financial future. And it's where I send you out—equipped, empowered, and encouraged—to go build the legacy God has called you to build.

Let me ask you one more time: do you believe that God has called you to build generational wealth? Do you believe that you have the ability, the creativity, and the faith to create something that lasts beyond your lifetime? Do you believe that you are an heir to the promises of God?

If the answer is yes, then let's finish strong.

Creating Your 100-Year Family Wealth Plan

Most people plan for the next paycheck. Some plan for the next year. A few plan for retirement. But almost nobody plans for the next hundred years.

A hundred-year plan isn't about predicting the future. It's about setting a direction that extends far beyond your own lifetime. It's about creating a vision so big that it requires multiple generations to fulfill it. And it's about putting the structures in place now so that your great-grandchildren have a foundation to build on.

Your hundred-year plan should include several key elements. First, a family mission statement. What does your family stand for? What are your core values? What is your God-given purpose? Write it down and revisit it regularly. This becomes the North Star that guides every financial decision your family makes.

Second, a wealth accumulation strategy. This is your plan for building assets—real estate, businesses, investments—that will grow and compound over decades. Think about what you can realistically build in your lifetime and what the next generation can add to it.

Third, a wealth preservation strategy. This includes your legal entities, trusts, insurance, and tax plans. These are the structures that protect your wealth from erosion and ensure it gets transferred efficiently to the next generation.

Fourth, a family governance plan. As your wealth grows, you'll need rules and processes for how decisions are made. Who manages the family trust? How are investment decisions made? Under what circumstances can family members access funds? These might seem premature now, but establishing governance early prevents conflict later.

Fifth, a legacy impact plan. What causes will your family support? What communities will you invest in? What change do you want to see in the world? Your wealth should be connected to a purpose that transcends money—something that makes your family proud and gives your resources eternal significance.

I know this might feel overwhelming. But remember—you don't have to build the whole thing in a weekend. Start with the family mission statement. Have the conversation. Write the vision. And then take it one step at a time.

The Power of Compound Legacy

You've probably heard of compound interest—the idea that money grows exponentially over time as the interest earned generates its own interest. It's one of the most powerful forces in finance. But I want to introduce you to an even more powerful concept: compound legacy.

Compound legacy is what happens when the values, knowledge, and resources you pass down to your children multiply in the next generation—and the generation after that.

Here's how it works. Let's say you start with nothing and build a net worth of five hundred thousand dollars in your lifetime. You teach your children everything you've learned. You give them a financial education, a strong work ethic, and a foundation of faith. Your children start where you ended. They don't have to build from zero—they build from five hundred thousand. With the same principles and strategies, they grow that to two million. And their children start at two million and grow it to ten million.

That's compound legacy. Each generation starts further ahead than the last. Each generation has more resources, more knowledge, and more opportunity. And over time, the growth becomes exponential.

But compound legacy only works if the transfer is intentional. If you build wealth but don't teach your children how to manage it, the compounding stops. If you create assets but don't create the structures to protect them, the compounding stops. If you accumulate resources but don't instill the values of stewardship and generosity, the compounding stops.

That's why every element of this book matters. The mindset. The strategies. The protection. The teaching. The community. The generosity. They all work together to create a compound legacy that grows stronger and richer with every generation.

You are the first link in a chain that could bless hundreds of people you'll never meet. Your children, your grandchildren, your great-grandchildren—they're all counting on what you do next. That's not pressure. That's purpose.

Your Final Assignment

Alright, it's time. Everything in this book has been building to this moment. You've got the knowledge. You've got the framework. You've got the faith. Now you need the commitment.

Here's what I want you to do in the next thirty days. Not the next year. Not someday. The next thirty days.

Week one: get your financial house in order. Pull your credit report. Calculate your net worth. Create or update your budget. Know exactly where you stand.

Week two: set your goals. Write your family mission statement. Define what generational wealth looks like for your family. Set specific, measurable goals for the next one year, five years, and twenty years.

Week three: take one strategic action. Open an investment account. Research a real estate market. Start a side business. Set up an LLC. Meet with a financial advisor. Do something that moves you from planning to doing.

Week four: build your community. Attend a real estate investment meeting. Join an online group of like-minded investors. Find a mentor. Schedule a family wealth meeting. Surround yourself with people who will support your vision and hold you accountable.

And every single day, pray. Pray over your finances. Pray over your family. Pray over your legacy. Invite God into every decision, every deal, and every dream. Because without Him, you can build something impressive. But with Him, you can build something eternal.

Look, you don't need all the answers right now. You just need to take the first step. Trust God, trust the process, and move forward. The perfect time to start is now.

I started this book by telling you that you were born to build. I want to end by telling you the same thing. You were born to build. You were called to create. You were designed to leave a legacy that glorifies God and blesses generations.

The world needs what you're about to build. Your family needs what you're about to create. And God is ready to partner with you in ways you can't even imagine.

So don't wait. Don't hesitate. Don't let fear, doubt, or procrastination steal what God has prepared for you.

This is your moment. Step into it with boldness, faith, and purpose.

You are an heir. Now go build like one.

I'm cheering for you. God's got you. And your legacy starts right now.

Reflection and Action Steps

This is it—your final assignment. But really, it's your first assignment as a legacy builder.

First, write your family's one-hundred-year vision statement. Where do you want your family to be financially in twenty-five years? Fifty years? One hundred years? Dream big. Write boldly. This vision will guide every financial decision you make from here forward.

Second, create your thirty-day action plan using the week-by-week framework in this chapter. Put specific dates on each action item. Share your plan with an accountability partner—your spouse, a mentor, a trusted friend—who will check in on your progress.

Third, revisit The HEIRS™ framework one final time. Rate yourself on a scale of one to ten in each area: Honor God First, Educate Yourself Relentlessly, Invest with Intention, Repeat and Scale, and Steward the Legacy. For any area where you scored below a seven, write down one specific action you'll take this month to improve.

Fourth, pray. Seriously. Get on your knees and surrender your financial journey to God. Ask Him for wisdom, courage, and faithfulness. Ask Him to open doors you can't see and close doors that would lead you astray.

Ask Him to bless the work of your hands and the legacy of your family.

And then stand up and get to work.

You've read the book. You have the knowledge. You have the framework. You have the faith. Now it's time to build.

You are an heir. Go live like one.

God's got you. And your legacy starts right now.

A Letter to Your Future Heirs

I want to close this book with one final exercise—one that might be the most meaningful thing you do in this entire journey.

I want you to write a letter to your future heirs. Not a legal document—a personal letter. A letter from your heart to the hearts of the children, grandchildren, and great-grandchildren who will one day inherit what you've built.

Tell them your story. Tell them where you started—the struggles, the fears, the moments when you almost gave up. Tell them about the first step you took after reading this book. Tell them about the first deal, the first investment, the first time you saw the fruit of your faith and hard work.

Tell them your values. Tell them what matters most to your family and why. Tell them about the faith that fueled your journey and the God who made it all possible. Tell them about The HEIRS™ framework and the principles that guided your decisions.

Tell them your dreams. Tell them what you hoped this wealth would make possible. Tell them about the communities you wanted to impact, the causes you wanted to support, the legacy you wanted to leave.

And tell them your charge. Challenge them to continue what you started. To steward what you built. To add to the foundation rather than consume it. To teach their own children and pass the torch with love, wisdom, and faithfulness.

Then seal that letter and put it somewhere safe—in your trust documents, in a family time capsule, or in a special place that your heirs will discover when the time is right.

That letter is more than words on paper. It's a bridge between your generation and theirs. It's a piece of your heart that will live on long after you're gone. It's the voice of a cycle-breaker, a wealth-builder, and a faithful heir speaking across time to the people they loved most.

Write the letter. Your heirs are waiting to hear from you.

And with that, I send you out. Not as someone who read a book, but as someone who is ready to build a legacy. You have the knowledge. You have the framework. You have the faith. You have the God who makes all things possible.

Go build. Go bless. Go leave a legacy that makes heaven proud.

You are an heir. Act like it. Build like it. Live like it.

God's got you. Now go get your legacy.

The perfect time to start is right now.

The Ripple Effect of One Decision

I want to leave you with one final thought—a thought that I hope stays with you for the rest of your life.

Every decision you make creates a ripple. A single decision to invest instead of spend creates a financial ripple that extends decades into the future. A single decision to teach your child about money creates an educational ripple that extends generations. A single decision to trust God with your finances creates a spiritual ripple that extends into eternity.

You may not see the full effect of your decisions in your lifetime. The property you buy today might be the foundation of your family's wealth for the next century. The financial conversation you have with your child tonight might shape how they manage millions of dollars someday. The tithe you give this Sunday might fund a ministry that changes thousands of lives.

That's the ripple effect. And it starts with one decision.

I think about my grandmother—the one I told you about in Chapter 1, counting her dollars behind the sugar jar. She never bought an investment property. She never started a business. She never had a financial advisor. But she made one decision that created a ripple through our entire family: she chose to be a faithful steward of what she had.

That decision taught my mother about responsibility. My mother's example taught me about stewardship. And my journey led me to real estate, to mentoring, to writing this book, and ultimately to you.

One decision. One faithful, ordinary, unglamorous decision by a woman who would never know the impact it would have. And here you are, reading these words, ready to create your own ripple.

So make the decision. Take the step. Trust God. And know that the ripple you create today will reach shores you'll never see—and bless people you'll never meet.

That's the power of one decision. That's the beauty of generational wealth. And that's why your legacy starts right now.

Go build it. I'm cheering for you every step of the way.

God bless you, heir. Now go claim your promise.

ACKNOWLEDGMENTS

First and foremost, all glory belongs to God. Without His guidance, provision, and faithfulness, none of this would be possible. Every lesson in this book, every breakthrough in my journey, and every word on these pages is a testament to His goodness.

To my family—thank you for believing in this vision even when it was just a seed. Your love, support, and patience have made all the difference. You are the reason I build.

To my mentors—thank you for pouring into me, challenging me, and showing me what was possible. Your wisdom is woven throughout these pages.

To every person I've had the privilege of coaching and mentoring—your stories, your courage, and your willingness to take action inspire me more than you know. This book exists because of you.

And to you, the reader—thank you for trusting me with your time and your journey. I don't take it lightly. I pray that the words in this book ignite something in you that can never be extinguished. Go build your legacy. The world is waiting.

ABOUT THE AUTHOR

Kito J. Johnson is a real estate investor, mentor, and faith-driven entrepreneur dedicated to helping individuals and families build generational wealth through practical strategies and biblical principles.

Starting with his first real estate deal at just twenty years old, Kito J. Johnson has built a portfolio of income-producing properties and mentored hundreds of people on their journey to financial freedom. His approach combines street-smart investing with deep spiritual conviction, making wealth-building accessible to people from all walks of life.

When he's not closing deals or coaching clients, you can find him spending time with his family, serving at his local church, and dreaming up the next big idea to help people win with money and faith.

Connect with Kito J. Johnson and join The HEIRS™ community at www.theheirsfamily.com.

www.ingramcontent.com/pod-product-compliance
Lightning Source LLC
LaVergne TN
LVHW020717110826
845149LV00012B/2299

* 9 7 8 0 9 9 8 9 5 0 2 5 9 *